Praise for
I Found *Myself* in China

称赞

PRAISE

With her truly inspiring tale of growth, Brinton draws from her own journey, offering hope to anyone wishing to redefine themselves, regain their sense of purpose, or reconnect with their confidence. An uplifting read for anyone in the midst of life's many unsettling transitions.

~ *Amanda H Young, author of* Finding Clarity, *founder and president of* Simplify Your Marketing

Once I started reading Joyce Brinton's *I Found Myself in China* I couldn't put it down, I just wanted more. Joyce is an inspiration and testament that if you believe you can make a difference in the world – through hard work and never giving up – you can.

~ *Tava Udall, business owner/entrepreneur*

I was hooked from Chapter One. Joyce delights in sharing her journey; from leaving the safety of her kitchen (to teach young Chinese women how to find self-confidence) to unexpectedly discovering her own passion in a foreign land. Hers is the most inspirational message I've read all year.

~ *Trish Walker, author of* Oh Honey…I'm Just Getting Started. Consciously Create Your Next Decade.

I Found Myself In China is a skillfully-written, true narrative of self-discovery that transports author Joyce Brinton from her routine life into an extraordinary woman who impacts thousands. Her reawakening is a model for anyone who wishes to live the life of which they once dreamed or for those who simply want a more fulfilling life. It's a story of becoming, with application to one and all. Including myself.

~ *Carlin G. Bartschi, M.D., retired emergency room doctor*

Joyce always carries herself with warm enthusiasm and cheer, which is the most valuable thing I learned from her while she taught me in China.

Joyce accelerates young college women leaders' self-development by providing excellent mentoring and coaching. I remember her taking care of hundreds of young women and men while she herself struggled in an unfamiliar foreign culture. She does what she says she will do and has a positive attitude while doing it. Personally, knowing her has been a wonderful and valuable part of my life. Born and raised in rural China, I would never have been able to attend one of the top American Universities to earn my MBA and then find my dream job without her continuous support and encouragement.

She is one of the most passionate people I know. I always wondered how Joyce could juggle her multiple roles of family, church, volunteering, and life coach simultaneously, but still find time to hang out with so many lifelong friends. This book tells how she makes it happen. I look forward to hearing more from this wonderful storyteller.

～ *Dan Dan Zhao, former student at The World Academy for Women*

Joyce grabbed me right from the beginning with her charm, wit, and vulnerability. I was right there with her self-doubt when she realized a big part of her life was done. However, the fun begins when she finds the inspiration to move on, and where that inspiration leads--to China, of all places!

～ *Dr. Dorine Kramer, retired infectious disease M.D. and author of* Your Amazing Itty Bitty Empty-Nesters Survival Handbook: 15 Critical Tips To Thrive When Your Kids Leave Home

Joyce Brinton coached me to find my inner power and my path to success. She guided me to pursue my vision, live a fully expressed life, and have my own voice. It's her that makes me want to meet a better me.

～ *Grace Liang, former student at The World Academy for Women*

Joyce Brinton's *I Found Myself in China* is an inspirational story that I thoroughly enjoyed reading. I related to what Joyce went through with her children and recalled my own emptiness in the same situation. Hers is truly a lovely story, packed with emotions, tears, laughter, and empowerment.

～ *Irene Freitas, Feng Shui Strategist, Energy Practitioner, Spiritual Coach*

Joyce brilliantly describes her own personal transformation when she chose courage over fear. She is a model for preparing and promoting women to live life bigger than they can imagine. And now she is sharing it with all of us!

~ *Jerrie Ueberle, Founder and CEO, Global Interactions and The World Academy for Women.*

Joyce is a role model for all women. Her drive to help grow the hearts and minds of those she touches is inspiring. Thank you, Joyce, for sharing your experiences with us!

~ *Pat Richardson, retired Commercial Lending Officer with Wells Fargo Bank*

Reading Joyce's book was like sitting down with a trusted friend to have an intimate conversation...delightful, tender and inspiring.

~ *Suzan K. Manning, M.A.P.C. M.Ed.*

I Found Myself in China embarks upon Joyce Brinton's poignant journey through fear and doubt to the ultimate destination of joy, empowerment and self-love.

~ *Danielle Cantin, President, Yes And Marketing*

I Found Myself in China

I Found *Myself* in China

A Journey to What's Next in Life

BEGINNING

Joyce Brinton

Surrogate Press®

Copyright ©2017 Joyce Brinton

All rights reserved.

No part of this publication may be reproduced, stored in a retrieval system, or transmitted in any form or by any means, electronic, mechanical, photocopying, recording, or otherwise, without written permission of the author.

Published in the United States by
Surrogate Press®
an imprint of Faceted Press®
Surrogate Press, LLC
SurrogatePress.com

ISBN: 978-1-947459-03-8

Library of Congress Control Number: 2017912211

Book cover design by: Danielle Cantin

Interior design by: Katie Mullaly, Surrogate Press®

To Steve for seeing me for who I am and helping me step into the best version of myself.

To Keira, Loren, Claire, and Hannah for being amazing human beings, the kids of my dreams, and for making my experience as a mom such a great adventure.

To all the students at The World Academy for Women for wanting more and creating space for me to teach.

Table of Contents

CONTENTS

Preface 1

Chapter 1: The Year I Left the Kitchen 5

Chapter 2: Overcoming Obstacles 12

Chapter 3: Something Bigger Than Me 20

Chapter 4: Teach Us Confidence 31

Chapter 5: Dream Big 37

Chapter 6: What's In a Name? 42

Chapter 7: The Magic of Miracles 48

Chapter 8: Transmit the Love 67

Chapter 9: I Am Amazing 72

Chapter 10: Who Defines Me? 79

Chapter 11: What's Next? 86

Acknowledgements 98

About the Author 100

Preface

PREFACE

Ever since I was five years old I talked about being a mom someday. I loved my little nieces that started being born around then (I was the youngest of six), and pretended they were my babies. I dressed them up and put them in my doll strollers and taught them to do silly things. The song I used to sing when I was little was *"When I grow up, I want to be a mommy and have a family, and serve cookies and milk and yellow balloons."* My mom was an awesome role model who made time for her kids, even after working a full time job. She canned, cooked, sewed and started a 4-H group for me. I wanted to be a mom just like her.

As the years passed, I decided to go to college at age 17, but I did not have a goal to finish. My main goal was to find a husband to be my knight in shining armor, someone to let me have babies and stay at home with them. (Today, it is a little embarrassing when I say this, but that was exactly where my mind was.) I dated a lot of great guys, got engaged four times (yes, I was a runaway bride), and finished my bachelor's degree in Communications without a plan or a husband.

A week after graduation I quickly took the GRE, and applied to graduate school in counseling, and within three weeks I was accepted. But just like when I was an undergraduate, I did not go into my graduate program thinking I would finish it. My boyfriend during graduate school became my fiancé and we planned for a wedding after graduation. One year into that relationship, I got cold feet once again and broke it off. I was in love with love and had one thing on my mind; *the idea of marriage.*

My last year in graduate school I taught a communications class and dated one of my students. He took it slow and we became good friends. My standing joke today is that my husband, Steve, was my student, and he waited until he got his A before he asked me out on a date. It was my last semester in graduate school when we started dating, and not long after dating we became engaged.

My sister sent Steve a cartoon from the paper with a girl and a guy at the courthouse getting their marriage license. The guy in the cartoon looked very happy; the caption had the woman saying, "Don't get too excited I've been here four times before." My sister wrote "I'll believe it when I see it." But this relationship stuck. We were married six months later, and I graduated the week after our wedding.

My job right out of school was at the State Mental Hospital and it was great. It included benefits, so I knew I could start a family anytime. Six months later I became pregnant with our first child. I still worked after this baby girl was born, but it was a job that allowed me to be home with her most of the time. Steve and I became head residents of the dorms on our college campus. He finished his graduate degree a few years later and we moved to Arizona.

My dream had come true! I was able to stay at home and be a mom. I became pregnant with our second child three years later, and planned the next two children to be three years apart each. After four kids I decided that was enough, and played stay-at-home mom for the next thirty years. I dedicated my life to our children. I loved every aspect of being a mom (excluding drivers' training, which scared me to death).

I spent hours each day looking for ways to enhance my children's lives and help them develop their God-given talents. I had a dancer, a drummer, an organizer, and a buddy in business ventures. Who could ask for more? My life was full and I loved it.

When my last daughter left for college I felt my heart being pulled right out of my chest. She and I cried and hugged and cried some more as we dropped her off at her apartment twelve hours away from home.

When my dreams of being a mom were fulfilled no one told me what happens when the kids leave home and they don't need me to be involved in their lives any more. It was a very rough awakening to a reality for which I was not ready. I had no idea who I was outside of being my kids' mom. I was lost, depressed and felt like life no longer had meaning.

It was not long after my youngest graduated from high school that I had the opportunity show up to go to China to teach at The World Academy for Women. My new life's adventures began the day I committed to go to China in September 2011 and have not stopped since. Being a mom was the best experience I've ever had…until I went to China. It is not to be compared to being a mom, but rather acknowledged as a divine hand directing me to meet another part of myself. I now understand the value and importance of seeing a new side of me, and letting my children do the same.

The following chapters are my experiences in discovering who I am outside of being a mom, a wife, a sister, a daughter, an aunt and a grandmother. They are my experiences of awakening to myself and my gifts. I share them with you now in the hopes they will awaken something in you that allows you to start your own new journey.

Joyce Brinton

The Year I Left the Kitchen
Chapter One

LONELY

To raise a child who is comfortable enough to leave you means you've done your job. They are not ours to keep, but to teach how to soar on their own.
— Author Unknown —

Food, Glorious Food

During the happiest time of my life I started every day with the same thought; *What will be on the menu today?* I did not run a soup kitchen, a specialty café, or even a food truck. I ran a home with a husband, four kids, a dog, a cat, an occasional lizard, and for four months out of the year, a grandma and grandpa. I was a stay-at-home mom, who enjoyed preparing healthy meals for my family, and I was good at it. It's what defined me.

Growing up, I watched my own parents feed *everyone*. I learned from both my mom and dad how to cook, and by age twelve I took on the responsibility of cooking our family dinners. My mom worked full-time and it was helpful if I had dinner ready when she got home. Eventually my parents even put me on their checking account so I could buy groceries.

The kitchen became my comfort zone even after I grew up.

When my own kids were little they would sit on the counter and help me put ingredients in the mixing bowl for homemade cookies. I guess the kids thought it was fun because we were doing something together. For me it was such a natural thing, it was my default. I got the title of "Cookie Mama" because I made cookies at least three times a week. Of course, it was the kids' responsibility to lick the beaters (I was never concerned about salmonella back then). We all ate so much cookie dough we weren't even interested in the cookies by the time they came out of the oven.

As the kids got older I encouraged them to ask for their favorite meals when I made a weekly menu: enchiladas, the good sandwich, antipasto salad, lasagna, and of course, dessert. On Sundays there was always a special dessert; on birthdays a favorite cake or pie; Christmas brought cake with cranberries; on Thanksgiving we had cream pies. It was important for me to make my kids feel special and I seemed to do that with food. I know there are books written about people with eating disorders and how they were loved with food. Well, that was me. I loved my kids with food. I think they felt special when I cooked for them. Thankfully, none of them are obese, so maybe just the love stuck.

Back then our house was what I called the Kool-Aid House, because I always had refreshments ready. I told everyone, "Feel free to stop by, there's always food and cookies to share." My motto was (and still is), *The more the merrier*. I could make up a meal in ten minutes, and have a batch of cookies baked in fifteen.

My oldest daughter's friends had open campus at lunch and they knew they were welcome in my kitchen. They would come in the house, open the fridge and eat their favorite leftovers or make a sandwich. It made me smile, and brought me a sense of satisfaction, like I was helping them in some small way.

Once a month I made a big dinner for my son and his friends. They loved it and I loved having them all there. I got to hear the stories of who was the latest hot girl they had a crush on and what their next game plan was for a mischievous escapade. Years later, when my son travelled in a rock band he would call me from another state and say, "Hey Mom, I have some friends in a band in town. Can they stay at your house?"

My answer was always, "Of course!" I made sure they had a good meal when they got in and I sent them off with a healthy breakfast. In appreciation, they always left me one of their CDs and respectfully cleaned up after themselves. It was at these gatherings where I heard stories about my son on the road that I would not have known otherwise.

My daughter was a dancer and I was the mom who brought healthy snacks to her all-day rehearsals. All my kids volunteered me to bring treats for the bake sales or classroom parties. When my two younger daughters wanted to make money, they started a bread business and took orders from neighbors and friends.

Yes, I was definitely a "foodie mom." I often said, "I think I have a neon sign on my forehead that says, *FOOD, open all day, every day*."

I must admit I loved being the house to which the neighborhood kids came to have food. Everyone who entered my home said, "Oh, it smells so good in here." There was always something cooking.

Looking back, my kids always showed up with friends, because they knew everyone was welcome. They knew I was prepared to feed extras. It was like magic when I cooked a meal for six, and then three more unexpectedly showed up, yet somehow, I stretched it out and fed everyone. My family referred to me as the Magician in the Kitchen.

The Secret Ingredient

But even though the kitchen was my domain, I knew food wasn't all my kids needed from me. I often asked myself, "*What more could I be doing for my kids? What are their gifts and talents that I can help them explore and expand upon? How can I help them gain confidence in themselves to go out into the world to make a difference? What can I do to make their childhoods fun? What is it I need to teach them now, and how can I better listen to them and understand their needs?*"

I bought a greeting card once to give a friend who is a teacher. It said, "Children are always the only future the human race has; teach them well." I never gave it to her. It's still in my possession, because that greeting card sentiment became my mantra.

As a mom, I spent most of my waking moments, and even occasional sleeping ones, thinking about my children and how to help them jump over the hurdles of navigating their lives. It was what made me feel complete. In my mind, I had the most important job on earth. It was up to me to make sure I equipped my children with what they needed to make good choices – choices that could make or break them.

And Then it All Came Crashing Down

Raising four kids and taking care of my family was the most rewarding time of my life. Watching my (really cute) babies grow up into amazing human beings who are (in my opinion) truly out there in the world serving, raising their own babies, using their talents, educating themselves, and enjoying life, is the most fulfilling thing I have ever experienced. Don't get me wrong, my kids are not perfect. They have their weaknesses and I have not been a perfect mother. I lived my life through them and the experiences they had. They were my sole purpose, consequently they needed to leave this clingy mother and get their own sets of wings.

And they did! Which suddenly left me without direction.

After thirty years of having these awesome children in my daily life, they each did something that shook me to my core; they moved on. Now it was their turn to go out into the world and strut their stuff. It is the most gratifying feeling to see them become unique individuals and grow into people who contribute to our future. I loved watching them evolve into grown-ups...that is until my last child decided to leave home.

Oh wait! She didn't decide to leave, *her dad decided for her.*

By that last comment, you can see that her leaving was not what I wanted. My last child was my sidekick. She ran errands with me, ran a food business with me, helped me in the kitchen – she was my own personal assistant. We were so connected that her father and I decided (yes, I was in on this decision) it was time she went to college *away* from home and spread her wings. Even though it was a joint agreement, I had such a difficult time accepting it. Fortunately, my husband was the one who helped her apply to colleges and (lovingly) pushed her out the door. It was one of the most painful things I have ever experienced. I knew it was the best thing in the world for her, but what was I going to do without her?

When all my children left home (as they should), I felt like I had been fired from the best job I'd ever had, *or ever will have*. After working for thirty years doing what I loved most; cooking, cleaning, teaching, loving, decorating, entertaining, nursing, training, playing, partying, diapering, encouraging, partnering, and dressing, now I had nothing to fill the void created when all that ended.

Now what? I thought. I loved my job as a mom, and I did it well. But now my children no longer needed me (at least not on a daily basis), and that hurt, especially when it came to the kitchen. Oh sure, my husband and I had to eat, but cooking for two has its limits, and it isn't as much fun.

The hardest time came when we dropped off my last child (my *sidekick* daughter) at college 600 miles from home. I had to say goodbye to one of my best friends. Everything inside of me screamed, *"NO! Just stick around for another 30 years, please!"* Everyone said it's best for her, and I knew it was, but it still tore my heart right out of my chest. I cried for days.

A week later she called and said, "What would you say if I wanted to come home?"

I started crying and handed the phone to my husband, because I knew I couldn't say no. His response to her was, "That is not a good idea, and it's not an option. There isn't much here for you. You need to stay there. You'll never grow up if you come home."

I wavered, knowing she was sad and lonely and wanted to come back to the comforts and stability of what she knew. I wanted the same thing.

I wanted the comforts of what I knew, which was raising kids. And if she came home, I could have that back.

Where the Trail Ends the Adventure Begins

Days later, I lay staring at the trees blowing outside my bedroom window, not wanting to get out of bed. I had no motivation. All I could think of was *why is it so quiet? Why can't I hear the voices of children anymore?* They brought me angst and joy. Their little fingers poking under the bathroom door and their voices crying out, "Mom, Mom! Are you in there? I'm hungry!" The fighting, screaming, demanding, giggling, those joyful little voices, the creaking noise from the front door of teenagers coming in at all hours of the day and night, hollering, "Mom, are you here? I'm home." All of that was no longer present.

Can I make them stay young forever?

One of the things I realized is I had failed to write the script for the third act of my life. The first act was a given: My childhood, adolescence, and college. The second was marriage and children. But for the third act, I had nothing; no plan, no dream, no aspiration calling me forward. I just wanted life to stay the way I knew it. "*Can I make a U-turn?*" I thought.

Even with my husband by my side, I felt completely alone once my children were out of the house, and I had no idea what to do. I felt like I was in a rowboat without oars, floating adrift in the Sea of Unknown. It was a very dark and frightening feeling. I know it was difficult for my husband and others to be around me, because I was in this hole and couldn't get myself out. I was embarrassed and tried to hide my depression, because I knew I had so much to be thankful for, even with my children grown and gone. *What the heck was wrong with me? Why couldn't I just pull myself up by the bootstraps and move forward and be happy? I have such a wonderful life!*

I had the life I always dreamed of. And I was grateful for it, grateful to my husband for providing me the opportunity to stay home and raise our kids. There was so much I learned during those mothering years. I realize now that I didn't just cook and clean. Skills emerged that I didn't know I had, because they just flowed out of me seamlessly out of necessity. All my compassion, patience, flexibility, creativity, inspiration, teaching moments, love, passion, and energy show up in my kids today even better than I could imagine. I love who they are and I feel so pleased when I see them living their lives passionately and energetically. They are who they are not because of me but because they chose to live passionate lives, learning, and seeking truths. They are my reward.

After they all left home, the question for me became, *Now what?* I had no idea what to do with the void I felt, and yet, deep inside, I knew I had a lot to offer the world. I just needed to figure out what that was exactly, and how to bring it out.

But for the time being, all I could wonder was, *Where is the adventure others speak of when the kids all leave home?*

Overcoming Obstacles
Chapter Two

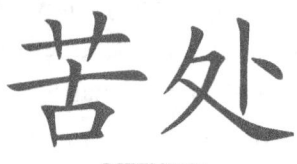

DIFFICULT

*Obstacles don't have to stop you.
If you run into a wall, don't turn around and give up.
Figure out how to climb it, go through it or walk around it.*
— MICHAEL JORDAN —

The pathway I knew so well of being a stay-at-home mom had ended, and I was in uncharted territory. However, I knew there was something inside me wanting to come out, but I had no idea what it was or how to get at it. I wasn't ready to put myself into storage. I longed to give to someone, somewhere.

There were a lot of emotions attached to this yearning. I was angry at myself for feeling sad, which I interpreted as ungrateful, mad at my kids for leaving, and mad at God for having them grow up! There was such a deep sadness and loneliness, I felt like I was sinking. Life was bland, like food without salt. The house felt like a morgue. The stillness and quiet was so haunting I had to play music or have the TV on at all times to keep me company. I seldom had the TV on when the kids were home, because it just added too much noise and chaos. Inside the dark hole of my mind (into which I was rapidly sinking), I screamed for help. *Someone please get me out of here!*

I didn't speak much about what I was feeling, because it felt foolish. *Everyone goes through this, what's wrong with me?* I know my husband sensed it and didn't know how to help (normally, he's a good fixer). At his wit's end, he invited me to attend a three-day seminar, hoping it would coax me out of my funk. He was excited and sat in the front row of the event. I, however, sat in the back row sulking and basking in my dark abyss. He kept enthusiastically turning around on breaks, motioning for me to come sit up front with him. I just couldn't muster up the energy to do it. In fact, what I really wanted to do was leave and come back later to pick him up. But I pushed myself to stay.

The instructor of the seminar presented a lot of good information. The one that got my attention was the use and power of vision boards. I had seen them before and shrugged them off saying to myself, "*Ugh, what is this going to do for me? It's just a bunch of positive affirmation crap. Besides, I can't come up with anything I want.*" The instructor asked us to write down one of our vision board statements and tape it up to the wall. I wrote, "*I want to know what I feel passionate about.*" I read others' statements trying to get ideas or steal theirs but nothing resonated with me.

I remained in the back row and continued to pout.

After we returned home, however, I decided to create and put up a vision board. I mean, what's the harm, right? I had nothing else to do, since my kids were all out living their own lives I needed to find a life, too. I had no idea what I wanted to do for my vision board, so I started to make stuff up. For example, I always wanted a Vita Mix blender. But every time I brought it up, my husband told me, "That's nuts! Who would pay $300 for a blender?" But this was *my* vision, so I put a picture of a Vita Mix on my vision board with the statement, "I own a Vita Mix." I also added other things like, "I go to the Philippines with my daughter," and "I have a wood floor in my family room."

Shortly after I created my vision board and put it up, my husband came home from Costco one day with…wait for it…a Vita Mix. After seeing a demonstration, he was sold. "I think we'd eat healthier if we had one," he said, and bought it. I'm so glad it was *his idea* and not mine.

One day, while my daughter was still at home, she was watching a documentary on BYUtv - Iris series entitled *Breaking the Curse*, and I decided to watch it with her. She knew I was struggling with what to do next in my life. It was about a woman whose daughter committed suicide at college. In the movie, the mom noticed, while cleaning up her daughter's dorm room that her daughter had been donating money to an orphanage in India. The mom had no idea her daughter had been doing this. At the funeral, she asked for donations in lieu of flowers and sent them to the orphanage in remembrance. As a result, the administrators of the orphanage invited the mom to India to see the orphanage for herself.

While in India she was shocked to see so many people stricken with leprosy begging in the streets. To her relief, the orphanage was doing fine, but it was the leprosy victims that tugged at her heart. She had been a stay-at-home mom and had never been outside the comfort zone of her life. She ended up going back to India a number of times and started a nonprofit business teaching leprosy victims how to have confidence and start their own businesses to make money so they did not have to beg.

This film inspired me. It left me with my heart pounding and mind racing with questions like, *What can I do to make a difference in the world? I knew I had something to offer, but what and where would I do that?* I had done volunteer work with women over the years in classes, shelters, or schools, helping them learn how to set boundaries and speak up for themselves. I decided that it was time for me to do this in other countries. The statement I put on my vision board was this: *I go to other countries and help women find their voices and take a stand for themselves.*

For the first time in months I felt excited about something. I thought *What if I really did that? That would be so cool.* Of course, I had no idea how that would happen but it boosted me out of my dark hole for a moment.

A Turning Point

Six months later, my friend Judi asked me to go to breakfast with her. We'd just dropped our daughters off for a weekend road trip with friends.

It was early in the morning, so we had both thrown on sweats, but had not yet brushed teeth or combed hair.

"Sure," I said, "I don't even have a bra on, but I'll go."

"Me, neither!" was her response. "But who cares?"

We laughed and met at a local café. While sitting in the restaurant, discussing what was next in our lives, she asked me this question: "Do you want to go to China and teach?"

My response was an emphatic, "NO, I don't want to go to China. That's a scary place. It is a communist country." But intrigued, I then asked, "What would we teach, anyway?"

"There's a woman from Phoenix who started a program in China," she said, "at SIAS International University called The World Academy for Women. They teach women to find their voices and take a stand for themselves, so they can make a difference in the world."

You can imagine my reaction when she said those words. I nearly fell out of my chair. I didn't look around me to see who was watching, I just started crying. My heart pounded wildly. I was scared, but captivated and said, "I have to go to China. That statement is on my vision board. Where do I sign up?"

Through tears she confessed, "I know what you mean. I have to go, too. Let's go together."

Three days later, Judi and I sat in Jerrie Uberle's living room finding out more about The World Academy for Women in China. I was anything but professional. While asking Jerrie questions I cried like a baby. I was embarrassed, profusely apologized, and claimed myself as a chronic crier. They were tears of inspiration more than anything else. Don't get me wrong, the whole idea of going to China scared me to death. I had no idea what I was committing myself to. It was as though a winch had hooked my heart and pulled me in the direction of China. I could not and did not want to unhook that winch. I asked Jerrie, "When do you need us there to teach?" She replied, "In five weeks, on September first."

It was the end of July, and I had a weeklong family vacation previously planned, plus I was already committed to attend a girl's camp as a chaperone for five days. My departure was five weeks away, and I still had to write a curriculum using PowerPoint (which I knew nothing about) on discovering your purpose and passion. *Did you get that? The classes I would be teaching were about discovering your passion.*

I had no idea what my passion was until the moment I was captivated by the idea of teaching women in China. I needed to purchase a plane ticket to China and get a visa.

I was overwhelmed and so fired up at the same time. Sometimes I can get into machine mode and get so many things accomplished. I don't even know how I did it. Judi and I worked at least three days a week on our curriculum. She was going to teach the second-year students and I would teach the first-year students. It was good for us to work together because we could pick each other up when the other was discouraged or blocked. Every day, at least five times a day, we would ask each other, "What the heck are we doing?" or "Why are we doing this?"

We had no idea except it was a big possibility that called, relieving us from the huge funk we both were in. Not only was I nervous, but the excitement level in my life grew so much I could not sleep at night. I would stay up until 3:00 a.m. working on my curriculum, and then wake up at 7:00 a.m. to get going again. The emotional roller coaster was beyond exhilarating. There were big highs and deep lows, but at least I was out of the emotional pit I had been in for so long.

Strangely, miracles started happening and doors opened, but obstacles also appeared. For example, I had no idea how to use PowerPoint, but I kept writing my curriculum anyway, in hopes I would find someone who did, and then they could help me create a slide how. And then sure enough, one day a woman who was a college professor from Missouri came to town to learn more about the women's academy. I hosted Ginger in my home and enjoyed making a new friend. The gift she brought me was she was proficient at PowerPoint. I wrote down on paper my

PowerPoint presentation and she helped me create my curriculum as a slide presentation. What a blessing she was!

Next, I needed to get a visa. Jerrie offered to help me with that, because I had no idea where to start. Traveling abroad was not something I had done before. I mailed my passport to Jerrie and a week later she had not received it! Taking a deep breath and working hard to not freak out I simply took a little day trip to Tucson and purchased a passport that was ready in 24 hours. Next I needed my ticket to China, but to purchase that I had to have a passport and a visa. Remember I only had five weeks to do all this, actually, only three because two of them were already committed.

The Miracles Begin

In 2008 I purchased a machine called an SE-5 for $2,800 in hopes I could help my family and friends improve their health. I am not fond of going to doctors so I like to use natural remedies that encourage healing without medicine. The SE-5 is a diagnostic machine that reads the vibrational levels and functions of the body. It identifies ailments before they move deeper into the body. It was fun to use at the time, and even helpful, but once the kids left home I found it catching dust more than being used. A few weeks before I had even heard about the China experience I called the company I purchased it from and asked if they buy back used machines. The lady on the phone said, "You can send it back to us. Sometimes people want to buy used machines and we will try to sell it for you." There was no harm in that because I hadn't used it in at least two years.

A week after I committed to go to China (not knowing how I would pay for my plane ticket, by the way) I got a phone call from the SE-5 company notifying me that my machine had sold for $2,000.00. This was the amount I needed to pay for a plane ticket and use for spending money while in China. This was just the beginning of miracles that answered all of my *Why's?* and *How's?*

There was no backing out of this commitment now. On many occasions, I wanted to say, "*I can't do this. It scares me and I don't know what*

I am getting myself into." I truly relied on miracles and the original decision I made to teach women to find their voices and take a stand for themselves. Not a single day passed in those five weeks that I was not petrified and questioned my sanity. I heard a quote somewhere that said, "Inspiration minus expression equals depression or discouragement." My six months or more of depression for having no purpose was suddenly kicked out, because I now had something purposeful in my life calling me forward, and it was bigger than anything I knew how to do. Every time I considered renegotiating my commitment, or not going at all, I became very depressed, worse than I was before. Pulling out of going to China was not an option. I had to keep moving ahead. Even the obstacles that popped up during my preparation did not discourage me. On the contrary, they almost encouraged me with such zeal or rebelliousness, as if to say "*Watch me. I will do this despite the setbacks."*

Leaving on a Jet Plane

The time had come. Before I knew it, Judi and I were on a plane headed to China. Saying goodbye to my husband for five weeks was not easy. I felt reassured that we could talk on Skype. My anxiety level was high, but so was my excitement.

We often said to each other, "Look at all the doors that opened and the serendipitous moments we've had so we could be here. There is no turning back now."

In the LAX airport we met a lovely Asian woman wearing a beautiful hat with a flower on it. She boarded our plane. When I commented to her how pretty her hat was she said, "It is a great way to cover up the bad hair after traveling twelve hours."

That was a good idea! I wish I'd thought of it. I was more concerned about my comfort and my ability to sleep on the plane rather than how I looked. My backpack was full of snacks, books, a computer, two blow up pillows, the rice filled U-shaped pillow for my neck and an extra blanket. All I was lacking was the floral shirt and camera to fit in with the other tourists. But no hat, or anything else, for that matter, that would improve my looks. I'm sure I was a sight to see, but I didn't care.

The lady in the hat deplaned in Beijing with us. I asked her where she was going. Her response was, "I have a program in Thailand where I teach women to gain confidence in themselves and have a voice."

Judi and I both looked at each other and started to cry, another serendipitous moment that reminded us we were in the right place at the right time. We got her business card and said, "Maybe we will go to Thailand next."

Something Bigger Than Me
Chapter Three

STRANGER

*Challenges are what makes life interesting
and overcoming them is what makes life meaningful.*
— Joshua J. Marine —

I was in Beijing, China. I felt like a stranger in a strange land, looking, grasping for something familiar, but elevated into something bigger than myself. It was a bit surreal to stand at my hotel window, and look out over the busy, smoggy city full of endless cars honking and weaving in and out of traffic, and people crowding the sidewalks. Once again, I asked myself, *What brought me here? What do I think I am doing?*

I was there because I said "yes," and then listened, acted, and did what it took to be there. Now let the games begin!

It did feel like a game, or a dream, or an illusion of some sort.

I had only been in China for four hours and I needed a cookie fix, mostly because cookies have always been my comfort food. I was out of my comfort zone big time and needed something to calm my anxiety levels down. My first stop was a bakery in the grocery store across the street from my hotel. They had a whole wall of different shapes and colors of cookies. Of course, I had to buy one of every cookie on the shelf. As I sat in the foyer of the hotel with my bags from the store, I tasted a sample of each cookie. I guess I was hoping for something that tasted like shortbread, because that's what it looked like. To my displeasure it was terribly bland with only a hint of sugar and not a tinge of butter. Gratefully there was a garbage can nearby, because they all ended up thrown away with one bite taken out of each. There is nothing like a warm chocolate chip cookie oozing with melted chocolate right out of the oven. That is what I was looking for, a cookie from home. They didn't know what they were missing here in China.

When I paid for things I didn't know if I was paying too much or too little or getting the right change, it looked like play money to me. When I paid for my first lunch at the hotel I opened my hand with bills and coins and asked them to take what I owed. I realized that was pretty trusting of me (or dumb), but I had no idea what each bill or coin was worth.

Another shock was when I ordered a glass of water with my meal and received a cup of hot water. Water is a big deal for me and I am never without a water bottle. This was definitely going to be an experience. All I could think to myself was, *"You are in for an adventure, Joyce."*

After a layover in Beijing, a little sightseeing and some rest, I was off to Zhengzhou.

Upon my arrival I stepped into the realm of fame. Who knew I would be famous in a city so far away, in a foreign country, and be treated so special by complete strangers. Four women from The World Academy for Women were waiting with flowers, gift bags, smiling faces, and open arms. My immediate thoughts were, *"Where am I and who are these lovely strangers who treat me with such appreciation and kindness?"* My heart was touched as I held back tears.

When I entered the dormitory where I was to spend the next five weeks, I was relieved to discover I had my own apartment, with a separate living area, a bathroom with a shower and a western toilet. What more could I ask for? I had a rude awakening when I sat down on my double size bed with a cream-colored duvet coverlet. *This really can't be true, can it?* It was as though I had sat down on a wooden bench. I looked under the blanket and saw that the mattress was about two inches thick and lay on a wooden plank.

"Wow, this is going to be interesting!" I thought to myself.

Later, one of the students asked me, "Is the bed too hard for you? I love hard beds."

I did not want to sound rude, so I simply said, "At home I have a nice thick soft mattress that I melt into. Is there somewhere I can purchase a thicker mattress?"

Her response was a typical one I soon grew accustomed to: "Yes of course, it would be my pleasure to take you shopping for one tomorrow when I get out of class."

It seemed the students were always more than happy to take me anywhere or help make my stay a positive and comfortable one. Out of gratitude for my sacrifice to teach there, they were committed to serving me and the other facilitators.

Not only were the beds a rude awakening, but the food took some getting used to, as well. Whenever possible, I ate in the foreign faculty cafeteria. The native chef tried to make something familiar so all the Americans who were there teaching would be happy. Meals were served buffet style and always had Chinese entrée options. Each day of the week was the same thing. For example, Mondays was hoagie sandwich night, Wednesday was Italian (a big hit), and Fridays we had leftovers. I was always grateful to have peanut butter and honey as a constant option for a sandwich.

One afternoon the faculty cafeteria was in a flurry because, it was hoagie sandwich day! The smell of homemade French bread wafted through the air and was a wonderful reprieve from the usual aromas. The smell of fresh bread was warm and delicious, but the meat was spam (not my favorite)! For lunch that day I had a whole plate full of hot French bread with soft margarine. It was comfort food at its best!

Jet Lag is Real

I had been in China for three days and my head hurt and body throbbed. I was consistently waking up at 4:00 a.m.! My body did not know (or care) what time it was. My feet were covered with blisters from walking everywhere. The shoes I brought were not made for walking, but they were cute with a two-inch heel (at home it was important for me to look cute). Being fashionable soon lost its appeal when comfort and practicality took precedence. The day before I left for China I stopped by a thrift store and saw a comfy pair of loafers I thought I would buy for casual days. They became my favorite daily shoes because they were flat and practical.

And then there was the bed. I still hadn't gotten a new mattress. By now my body ached from sleeping directly on a wooden board. My bed was the size of a double and had a nice soft bedspread, which was deceiving at first glance. However, it did not cushion the hardness of the bed. After tossing and turning, trying to find a comfortable position, there was no doubt, I needed to buy another mattress!

On Friday evening as promised, my student "handler" (as they call them) showed up at 7:00 p.m. dressed in a cute ruffled dress and boots with fringe on the sides. She was a senior, and looked as though she had a hot date. When I asked her, "Are you going out with friends tonight?"

She quickly put her arm in my arm (this is common in China) and said, "You are my date tonight. I will take you shopping to get anything you need." What a relief it was to have my very own shopping partner to help me translate and do basic things like decipher body lotion from hair conditioner, body shampoo from hair shampoo, and bargain with the store owners on the purchase of a mattress for my bed. She even helped me safely cross the street. To me there were no traffic laws and pedestrians definitely did not have the right of way. As I stepped in front of a car to get to the other side of the street (thinking the driver would stop), my student handler grabbed my arm and said, "I need to teach you how to walk in Chinese traffic!"

During our shopping adventure, we chatted the whole time and I learned a little about her. She was from a small town by the sea, an only child whose parents were fishermen. Her mom and dad worked hard to send her to college, because they had very little education themselves.

She was "changing her stars," as I call it, by stepping out of how she was raised and doing something different.

Wait, I thought, *isn't that what I am doing? I am changing what I have known for the past 30 years in a drastic way.*

She was a second-year academy student and told me, "Before I was a member of the Women's Academy I was very shy, and had no confidence. Now I am confident, I take every opportunity that comes my way and I have become a great leader. A year ago, I was none of those things. Now I speak up and stand up for myself."

Needless to say, I was very impressed. In that moment I remembered I had written on my vision board that I would help women have a voice, and she was a product of that. I could see how the words on my vision board were playing out. I was there to be a guide, to help women get exactly what my new friend told me she had achieved. The people I met on campus were generous, loving and grateful to have foreign teachers there. The women in the academy treated us like royalty. I cried tears of gratitude for the experience of change. I was looking for a shift when I stepped out of my kitchen and motherhood. I knew something bigger than me led me to China. I wasn't sure what that was or why, but I was there now, and refused to leave until my five-week teaching commitment was up. I planned to give it all I had.

The Hard Part

But I missed my husband and kids *so much*. I wanted to talk to them and share with them everything I saw and experienced. The first thing I wanted to do when I got settled into my room was get Internet access so I could call home. It took me three days to get the correct hook-up supplies and someone to help me get online. It felt like weeks before I could talk to my family. I wanted to see their faces, listen to their voices and hear what the grandkids were doing. One of my daughters was pregnant with my first granddaughter. She was due shortly after I returned from China. I was anxious to see how she was feeling. My husband carried the load working, running the house, dealing with our finances, and being there for family while I was gone. I was so grateful that he supported me. I wanted him to know everything I experienced.

There were many lonely nights when I went to bed crying, and stayed awake into the night trying to get on the Internet so I could talk to someone from home. In the middle of the night I took my computer downstairs to the cafeteria where there was Wi-Fi. All the lights were out and I sat at a table with my phone flashlight trying to get online to check my emails. When I saw nothing from home I felt even worse. I thought, *Have they forgotten me? Why haven't they sent me an email or something?* I went back to my room and sobbed.

At that moment I was beyond sad. I was afraid, and questioned myself for being there. My pillow was wet from tears, and they were not tears of inspiration. I longed for home. I wanted to give in, give up and go back to America. It was too hard and I just didn't want to do it anymore. I have never done well being alone, and I was genuinely alone and very far away from the place I knew best – home.

Things were not as easy for me in China. The Internet was dial-up, sometimes it worked, but often it didn't. In order to print anything I had to download it onto a flash drive and take it to a print shop on campus. Trying to play charades with the print shop employees to communicate was entertaining to them and me. I remember standing in the print shop handing my flash drive to the assistant and pointing to the computer screen as he pulled up my documents. We looked at each other. He asked me something in Mandarin and I shrugged my shoulders. We both smiled and when we found the document I wanted I nodded my head *yes* and wrote down a number of how many copies I needed. It felt like a game. They always chuckled when I entered the shop looking for help.

My drinking water came from a water filter machine out on the wall in the hallway of my dorm, which was hot. Water was a big concern for me and I was grateful to see we had a place to get purified water even if it was hot. I filled my water bottles at night and put them in my refrigerator so they would be cool in the morning.

The water temperature was regulated by the main dormitory control system. The hot water in my shower was turned off by 9:00 p.m. and then turned back on in the morning from 7:00 a.m. to 9:00 a.m. I took a walk each morning and rushed back for a hot shower, but seldom made it in time, so I got used to taking cold showers.

The laundry facility in our dormitory was not the cleanest place to hang out. The washing machines were old and looked pretty dirty. The room was filled with piles of laundry lying on the (not so clean) floors. Lint from the dryers was thrown on the floor because the garbage cans were overflowing. After doing a load in the machines my clothes looked dirtier than before I put them in. I decided to hand wash my clothing in a large bowl in my shower. It became an evening ritual. Rather than let my dirty clothes build up in the laundry basket like I did at home I would wash them at the end of each day and hang them to dry. What can I say? *It is an adjustment, Joyce. Remain flexible and let things unfold.*

Am I Running?

I saw a quote on the Internet that said, "Travelling isn't always about running away from things, sometimes it's about running into what you truly want." This quote was fitting for me because I have often referred to myself as a runner. Not in the physical sense, but running from things. My husband calls me a "flight risk." When things get tough I want to run away. Some of my usual "fleeing" destinations included movies, friends' homes, shopping, I would go to Colorado to visit family, getting lost in books, and eating ice cream and cookies. I was always looking for a safe place to hide from pain, especially when my home was empty. I didn't know where to go, but I certainly needed something. China was not my typical destination; in fact it was a long shot from where I'd retreated before. I often wondered, *Should I have taken a cruise with my husband or gone on a fishing trip to Alaska?* It was not Disneyland or a nice resort in the Bahamas that's for sure! I did not know this call inside me to travel to another country was actually what I truly wanted. It just called to me from within and I answered, "Yes."

I had no idea what I was running from, or to, but I felt like I had won the race, mostly because I felt courageous for being there, and bold for pushing through the hoops to do so. I pushed beyond things I thought I could, or ever would, do. I liked the comforts of my home, my food, my bed, my daily schedule and my life. My job as a mother was familiar; it was what I did for thirty years. That job ended and my new position as a facilitator teaching women in China was just beginning.

The Discomforts

When I first stepped out of the van from the Zhengzhou airport the scent in the air was anything but desirable. I was trying to be nice, but I am sure my nose turned up and my eyebrows furrowed when I took in a breath. The air was a mixture of Chinese food cooking, fried oil, sewage, garbage, exhaust fumes, burning grass and coal. The University campus at which I taught was in the city of Xinzheng, a rural community surrounded by farms. It was autumn and the harvest was over so they were burning their fields. The air quality was very poor, both visually and on the nose. On certain days I could hardly see the sky because it was so smoky. It may sound like an insignificant problem to be so bothered by the air fragrance, but it definitely took some getting used to. I often felt nauseous as soon as I walked outside.

There were food carts lining the streets outside of campus that had various food items for sale. The fear of getting sick kept me from purchasing any street food. The smell alone was so unpleasant I had no temptation. There was a dish in particular that wreaked havoc on the nostrils, and it was called stinky tofu. It was just what the name implied. When I walked past it I fanned the front of my face and held my breath until we were far away from it before I would breathe again. The unfamiliar foods, living conditions, traffic laws (or lack thereof), the language barrier, and the smells were just some of the adjustments I had to make.

Maybe it's because I have always cooked and like my home cooking, but the food in China definitely was not my favorite thing. I am not a big meat eater to begin with, and when I do eat meat I like it boneless. I admit, I am a bit privileged and never really thought about that until I ate a bowl of soup with chopsticks. The meat in the bowl was full of small bones. The thought that I quickly had to put aside so I wouldn't get sick was *I hope this wasn't someone's pet.* One time I pulled a whole chicken head out of my soup. When we ordered fish, it was served whole. Yes, the whole fish, with skin, tail, bones and eyeballs staring me in the face. The students said, "When the fish faces you it will bring you good luck." I would've settled for a filet. I'm embarrassed to admit these inconveniences were so difficult for me. Mostly it was the unfamiliar. It wasn't home and I wasn't at ease.

On one particular evening after class I stepped into my shower (it resembled one you see in a motor home) and the nozzle fell off and hit my head. Unfortunately, it was one of those discouraging nights when I couldn't get the Internet working. I was hot and sweaty from teaching in a muggy classroom and I still needed to do my laundry. I lay down on my bed and cried. I wanted to go home. *Why did I sign up for this?*

There were a lot of inconveniences and discomforts that would have and could have stopped me. I had to get used to taking cold showers (once they fixed the nozzle), brushing my teeth with bottled water, not flushing toilet paper down the toilet, and even using squatty potties on campus. But one of the hardest adjustments for me was always feeling like I was on. From the moment I was picked up at the airport and transported to campus I became the students' mentor and teacher. And in turn, they treated me like a rock star. Every time I was out of my dorm room I was with a student or around students who were filled with wonder. They wanted to visit with me, be with me, ask questions and invite me to speak somewhere for something. There was never much warning when they asked. One evening one of them told me, "You will be the main speaker tomorrow morning at our *Stand Up and Make Noise* parade and lead the parade across campus." I thought, "*Okay, Joyce, you can do this.*" I hid behind the doors of my home, which was my domain. I could plan and predict my days most of the time. It's what I knew and had grown accustom to. I didn't have that comfort in China.

Another time a young lady said, "We would like you to speak at our Mothers Tea this afternoon and share your experiences at the academy with us." One of the students who had a film class asked me, "Will you be one of the actors in our film today? I will give you the script."

I am one who likes to think things through a little bit before I speak, teach, or perform. There wasn't much time to do that when the requests came in so quickly and randomly. This is what I mean by saying I felt like I was always *on*.

In my dorm room, however, I let myself relax a bit. But still, I knew I was never sure what would come next.

My Commitment

When I originally committed to go to China to teach at The World Academy for Women I did not stop to think, or plan out, what it would be like. I refused to let people tell me anything negative about China for fear it would stop me. There wasn't time to do research on where I was going, and it wouldn't matter even if I did. It grabbed me from the moment I heard the motto of The World Academy for the Future of Women was, "We teach women to take a stand for themselves, and have a voice to make a difference in the world." There was no stopping me at that point, the decision was made. My whole purpose and focus was to be all I could for those women and teach them what they wanted to be taught. I had no idea what was in store for me personally while I was there.

With all the upsets and inconveniences I felt a little discouraged, but not deterred. I asked myself, *How could I possibly quit on these women who depend on me*? If I gave up I'd be beyond disappointed in myself.

People live through tougher things than this and their hard experiences transform their lives. *Is it possible that I was about to give up a personal transformation just because I was unhappy and uncomfortable?*

Something inside of me profoundly answered all those questions. *No way girl, you are not going home. You will stay until you finish, get what you came here for, and give what you came to give!* I found a quote by George Bernard Shaw that seemed fitting for what I was experiencing and hung it on my bedroom wall. It said: "*I am of the opinion that my life belongs to the community, and as long as I live, it is my privilege to do for it whatever I can.*" I want to be thoroughly used up when I die, because the harder I work, the more I live. Life is a "brief candle" to me. It is a splendid torch that I get to hold for only a moment. I want to make it burn as brightly as possible before I hand it to future generations. Every morning when I woke up I read George Bernard Shaw's quote, and then said to myself; *I've come a long way from home to sit back, watch and complain. It is my privilege to be here and serve the women in the academy. I will let my light shine and be a beacon for them to follow, live fully and be used up when I depart.*

Teach Us Confidence
Chapter Four

COURAGE

The best way to gain self-confidence is to do what you are afraid to do.
— Swati Sharma

It took a few days to get over jetlag and settle in. Once that happened, I was ready to brave my new world on my own. I took a walk across campus. It was beautiful! At one time, it was a lotus field. There were large trees in little forests and green grassy areas on which to sit. It was built next to a river. In the middle of campus was a large pagoda surrounded by a lovely forest. The president of Sias University (which is the campus on which the Women's Academy resides) was a Chinese-American named Shawn Chen from Pasadena. His philosophy was to bring the world to the students, because most of them being from rural villages may never see anything outside of China. The architecture of the buildings represented different parts of the world. The entrance to campus was called European Street and had buildings that mirrored those from countries of Western Europe. For example, there was French, German, Italian, Russian and Spanish Squares. Italian Square was filled with shops and had white marble pillars in front of each one, with statues and fountains replicating architecture from Italy.

As I walked through Italian Square a student approached me and said, "Hello are you a facilitator for the Women's Academy?"

I responded with, "Yes I am, are you a member of the Academy?"

She replied, "Yes. This is my first year and my English is very poor. I look forward to learning from you. My name is Amber." I said to her, "You are very brave to approach me and introduce yourself when you don't feel confident with your English skills. You are the first student I have met on campus; therefore I will call you Amber One." With this first introduction of the caliber of students I would be teaching, I was impressed with her courage and wondered if they were all like this.

She seemed pleased as she shyly giggled and waved goodbye, adding, "I am so happy to meet you and will see you in class."

The First Class

When I entered my classroom I immediately noticed it had noisy, squeaky ceiling fans, trash on the floor, and rows of wooden desks crammed closely together, before I made a judgment I wisely realized that I was in the space of my student's treasured college setting. Most of the women in the Academy came from rural villages and families that had little, if any, education. This was a rare and wonderful opportunity for them, not only to be at college, but also to be a member of the Women's Academy. Their enthusiasm filled the air like children on Christmas morning. They giggled, chatted and their eyes glistened with zeal. They felt privileged and grateful to be there.

To be a member of the Women's Academy they had to go through a rigorous interview and application process. Only 100 students were chosen out of about 300 applicants. When I stood up in front of these beautiful faces all I felt was love and appreciation. I asked the students, "What do you want from me? What do you want me to teach you?" One small woman (they are all mostly small) raised her hand and said very meekly with her head bowed, "Teach us confidence."

I smiled and thought to myself, *Five weeks ago, I didn't have any self-confidence. I had no idea what I wanted to do with my life. I had lost my purpose. How ironic is it that I now stand in front of these Chinese women who beg me to teach them confidence?"*

I wasn't sure how confidence could be taught. I didn't think it could be read in a book or handed over with a compliment. But thoughts came to me as I stood there watching them anxiously awaiting my teachings. My confidence had been strengthened in the past five weeks from doing things that were not easy for me to do. That is what I would teach them, to do hard things. I found my new purpose. These students needed me and I had something valuable to give them. I immediately said very confidently, "Okay, that's what I'll teach you. Stand up straight, raise your head high, smile, walk around this classroom and introduce yourself to someone you don't know, then sit by them."

There was a lot of giggling and shy hand gestures going on while they did this, but it was a beginning.

Their homework assignment was to think of three things they wanted to accomplish but were afraid to do. They had thirty days to accomplish those three things and report to me. Within two weeks I started getting reports from students in class and on my email. One student talked to a photographer because she wanted to learn photography. Another student wanted to talk to the President of the University and did so in an open forum where he was speaking. This was the start of Confidence Lesson 101. I took the assignment myself and tried new foods, learned some Mandarin words, and rode a bicycle in traffic (which was very scary, and in my opinion life threatening). I had the students play a get-to-know you game that included dancing. This was a difficult thing for most of them to do, since many of them had never danced before. Their homework assignment was to go back to their dorm and practice dancing. One of the women asked if she could come to my apartment and have me teach her how to dance. I decided to make a party out of it and invited them all over to my dorm building Friday night, and we would have a dance party on the rooftop patio outside the laundry room where the clothesline hung.

"What does it look like to be confident?" I asked them.

One student responded with, "It is strong, successful, and beautiful like you."

I responded with honesty, "I have not always looked like this. I struggled with confidence recently and coming here to China has given me reassurance. For example, I didn't even know how to create a PowerPoint presentation or write my curriculum, but I received a lot of help in doing so. Now I know I can do it. I had many obstacles I had to overcome to get here and that gave me confidence as well."

One of the women kindly said, "I am so proud of you. The world is a campus and there are many teachers. I thank you for coming to be our teacher and doing things that were hard for you."

As usual tears ran down my cheeks when she spoke those words. I was willing to let myself be open and vulnerable if it helped my students. I knew my experiences were beneficial teaching tools that could act as a catalyst to their growth.

However, the students had a difficult time when I cried, it made them uncomfortable. They usually pulled out their tissues and tried to comfort me. I told them, "These are tears of inspiration; they are tears that brought me out of my discomfort and all the way to China."

I had done hard things in preparation to get to China, and I was doing hard things the moment I stepped into the unknown and listened to where my heart led me. My theory, or excuse, in life used to be, "I don't do hard things intentionally. I deal with things as they happen, but never sign up for the difficult stuff, like running a marathon, asking for a trial, or putting myself in uncomfortable places just for the growth of it."

But here I was in China, teaching confidence after having struggled with my own lack of self-esteem for the past year. I went from being depressed, wondering what my purpose was, and hiding wherever I could, to teaching confidence to these marvelous women. I signed up for this uncomfortable, unfamiliar, foreign experience and was so glad I did! I did it by being bold enough to listen to my intuition, when it was ignited the moment I heard about the Women's Academy. I stood powerfully with my decision even when it became difficult. I knew I had more to give and wanted to make a difference on this planet.

Teach Us Confidence

The desire was there, the opportunity came and I took a leap of faith.

Doing Whatever It Takes

I taught my Women's Academy classes four nights a week. The students were required to attend two of them a week, a coaching class every Friday and a weekly lab as an extracurricular noncredit activity. Three weeks into the classes I noticed Amber One (the very first student I met) attended every evening class and two or three coaching classes. I asked her, "Amber, do you know you are required to attend only two evening classes a week and one weekly coaching class?"

Amber's response was, "Yes I know that, but I want to come every night because I want to learn all I can from you. You are only here for a short time and I have already learned so much from you, and my English has improved."

Speaking through my tears (of course) I said, "You are always welcome to attend every class. I love having you here. You have touched my heart deeply."

Time Flies

I had been teaching about three weeks when I told my students, "Thank you for being so wonderful, hungry, and eager to learn. It is such a pleasure to teach you. You are truly model pupils. I am inspired each day I get to share my knowledge with you."

A lovely young lady who stood about five feet tall raised her hand, quickly stood up, shook her fist firmly in the air and loudly said to me, "We are not hungry, we are thirsty, and we will drink every drop of knowledge you give us."

That comment hit me like a lead hammer right in the chest. It was beyond anything I had ever experienced. I found my new mission right then and there. These women needed me to teach and that's what I would do with all my heart. My response to her was, "I will give you everything I have."

At the end of my five-week stay the original shy, beautiful, nervous women I first met no longer existed. They exhibited confidence daily—in class, on campus. Many of the foreign faculty members who I ate meals with in the cafeteria commented on the high caliber of the women students from the Academy. One of their English teachers said, "In my class I can always tell who is a member of the Women's Academy. These students ask great questions, make thoughtful comments, and are more professional. Whatever you are teaching them, the whole school needs more of it."

I had to agree.

Who would've known that this little mom and housewife from Arizona who had lost her way and hid her light could find it in China teaching women how to speak up for themselves *with confidence*? It was such a surprise for me to take inventory of what I was doing and the outcome I saw in my students. My own confidence grew as I taught them. What I was doing was something I had never imagined I would, or *could*, do. I saw I was making a difference in these women's lives.

And they were making a difference in mine.

Dream Big
Chapter Five

POSSIBILITY

*Hold fast to dreams for if dreams die,
life is a broken winged bird that cannot fly.*
— LANGSTON HUGHES —

When you have a dream, write it down or speak it. If you don't, you won't give birth to it. Originally, I underestimated the power of vision boards and how they open up possibilities for what seems impossible. Six months after I wrote on my vision board, "I go to other countries and empower women to take a stand for themselves and have a voice," I was in China doing that very thing. How did that happen? I wrote it down and I shared it with people I knew. *I owned it.*

When it was time to teach the women of China how to expand or recapture *their* dreams, I found myself remembering how much I had grown as a result of following through with my dreams. The theme of the first module I taught in China was *Discovering Your Purpose and Passion*. This was the perfect topic for me to be teaching as I was discovering my own new purpose.

One of my students, Grace, contacted me the second week I was there and said she needed to talk to me about my PowerPoint slides (she translated them for me). When we met she was excited and skeptical at the same time. Her questions consisted of, "How can miracles happen if we don't just work hard and make them happen? How can I dream if my dreams were shut down so many years ago? How do we listen to our hearts when I have been taught to listen only to my head? I don't understand what miracles are."

I said to Grace; "These questions are great, because the more you ask for, the more you will receive." It got me even more excited to see where we would go in class. If this was what one student was brave enough to ask, I wondered where and how the other students were stuck in pursuing their dreams.

Grace had always dreamed of becoming an international nurse. Her freshman year she started studying for her English exam and looking for ways to study nursing abroad. People around her told her it was impossible, she would never be able to do it, so she should just give up on that idea completely. She became very discouraged and buried that hope down deep inside. When I taught her she could dream again she was ecstatic and nervous all at the same time. "Nothing is impossible," I told her. I then followed up with "Don't let people tell you to give up on your dream."

She wrote that down and put it on a beautiful blue piece of paper I gave her for her vision board. A week after she wrote down, "I go to America to become an international nurse," her uncle called her and said, "I know you have always wanted to go to America to study. When you are ready to go I will give you a free flight using my airline miles."

Three years later, Grace was able to accept her uncle's gift and go to the United States to do an internship at a hospital, which was her first step to attending an American university in the future.

More Dreams and Visions

When I asked the women in my class to dream big, beyond their wildest dreams of what was possible for them, I was surprised to hear what they had to say. One of them said, "I want to buy my father a warm coat to wear in the winter." Another said, "I want to get my mom a pair of comfortable shoes and a soft chair to relax in when she comes in the house from working in the fields." These all seemed so kind and thoughtful. Their dreams consisted of serving their parents.

But after ten of the women shared, one stood up and declared, "I want to live on the beach in California."

The whole class giggled. I smiled and said, "Now you're dreaming big!" This student's name is Selia. She spent a considerable amount of time with me and shared a lot more of her dreams. She grew up in extreme poverty, and had to attend school away from home at a young age because there wasn't a school in her village. The living conditions and classrooms were extremely unpleasant and unbearable. Her major was education and she wanted to start her own school where students would have a comfortable learning environment and feel safe. She was about to quit school her senior year in college, because her parents, family, and friends could no longer support her. Different teachers and facilitators pitched in and tried to help her finish her schooling.

Then one day, an American businessman spoke at a symposium on campus and Selia was asked to translate for him (her English skills were exceptional). I told her to share her dreams with him.

She did.

And when she was finished the American businessman met with the director of our Academy and asked, "How can I help her? She is a remarkable woman and has wonderful dreams and ideas."

The director told him, "Selia needs her senior year paid for and an internship."

The American businessman said, "I can do that. I will pay her senior year and give her an internship with my company."

Nine months later Selia was in Huntington Beach, California doing an internship! She is currently in Palm Beach, Florida, finishing her Master's Degree and was accepted at Florida State for her Doctorate. When she first arrived in Florida she realized her campus was far from where she lived. When she called me, and said, "I have put on my vision board that I have a car and a driver's license by November." It was mid-October when she sent me a picture of her in front of a used car she purchased and had her license and car insurance.

She also put on her vision board that she travels abroad.

By spring break, she had visited Columbia, Cuba, and London. She looked for the cheapest places to go and people to stay with and went on faith.

Things happen when we set our visions bigger than what we know how to do. It is how we gain access to miracles.

Does it Really Work?

Even after my five-week teaching assignment was over and I returned to Arizona, I still received emails from my former students in China saying things like, "I was able to get a job on the holiday and I bought my mom a pair of shoes!" Another said, "I got my father a coat and he loved it." My student, Gloria, wanted to get her MBA in the United States, and she put that on her vision board. Her parents had never received a formal education, but supported her dreams as much as they could. Currently Gloria is in Phoenix in the MBA program at Arizona State University. She told me, "I did not know how I would possibly be able to pay for my tuition, but I knew I had to do it. I came and believed it would all work out."

And it did work out. She receives income through tutoring, translating and scholarships. Her words when she first arrived in America were, "I feel like I am in a movie. It was just a dream and now it has come true."

Another young lady, Dan Dan, approached me my first week on campus and visited with me about wanting to go to a Christian school in America. I introduced her to different universities in the U.S. as well as some Christian ones. She set her sights on Brigham Young University. Today she is an MBA student at BYU and she says, "I would love my brother to come to America to a university because it is a blessed land with freedom and so many opportunities." Another item she wrote on her vision board was, "I visit Europe to further my education." Shortly after that she received a scholarship to a study abroad in Europe for summer 2017.

I have students who have attended universities in London, Germany, France and those who have found wonderful jobs in Shanghai and Beijing. They believed in my belief in them. Because of that, they trusted that anything was possible. I received many emails after I left thanking me for simply believing in them. They did not give up on their dreams. Instead they pushed, pursued and were not afraid to share their dreams with others.

When my students told me that I taught them how to dream again, I recognized that my own hopes and visions came to pass. Being able to ignite or rekindle passion where it had been smothered brought me such joy and fulfillment that I knew I had found a niche for myself. This is how I wanted to spend my time and energy. I found my purpose, which is teaching others how to capture (or recapture) their visions of what they want for themselves. This has become *my* passion.

It's hard to believe now that I started out with no vision of what I wanted or where I would go or how I would serve. My beloved life as a stay-at-home mom ended, and my thoughts told me that my life ended, too.

In reality, my life had just begun.

I learned in order to find what I was passionate about I had to allow myself to be vulnerable, step into the unknown, learn along the way, persevere, dodge the fast balls, look for opportunities, open doors, and express gratitude. Staying in China when things got tough was the best thing I ever did. I still had occasional teary, lonely nights, but I broke new ground in my life, as well as in the lives of others.

And that made it all worth it.

What's In a Name?
Chapter Six

POTENTIAL

What's in a name?
That which we call a rose by any other name would smell as sweet.
— William Shakespeare —

When a baby is born we give it a name and a nurse places an ID bracelet on its leg with one that matches the mother's. We come into the world and receive a name that identifies us the moment we are born. A name is simply what it implies; a starting point in life. The rest is up to us.

Sometimes people don't like their names or relate pain with the name they have been given, so they change it. Some just want to have a nickname for fun or to be different. Sports players, for example, have nicknames, as do famous song writers, authors, and actors. I had one, too. Mine was Juice. My brother gave that to me when we were young and it stuck with me throughout college.

We don't have to get trapped in the identity of our names or what someone labels us. Many children are tagged these days as ADHD, ADD, autistic or ODD. Sometimes when they receive such a label they either grow into it or organically become it. A name can be a way to identify us, but we get to choose how to make it our own.

One of the greatest realizations I had in China was that I could change. I wasn't stuck in the conversations of "This is just how I am and how I have always been. People will just have to get used to me this way." Have you ever said that to yourself? Being in China made me realize that I didn't have to be the one who compared myself to others, hide my voice and step back, or feel intimidated. My identity changed on that trip. I had the same nametag, but not the same description I had worn for so many years. I was no longer Steve's wife, Evan's sister, or my children's mom; those were identities I gave to myself or were assigned to me by someone else.

Now I was Joyce with a powerful message to share.

Names are not just given to us for the convenience of calling out to each other. Names contain power that we can use to call forth the parts of ourselves we aspire to be. There is a freedom in assigning names with what we feel. For example, when we confront things like fear, anger, and shame, those negative emotions lose power over us. It loosens their grip. The same thing holds true for our given names. You don't have to align your name with your identity unless you choose to. You can surrender to your name or let it go. My students wanted to live into their names, because to them doing so was a beautiful way to identify where they were going and who they would be.

Student's Chinese Names

One evening, I sat on the bed in my room and chatted with six students about who we were and how we become who we want to be. During the conversation we talked about the history of China. Each town the women were from had a special distinction and they each said, "My city is very old and famous." I felt the history everywhere I visited. It is taught in the schools and evident throughout the country. The students have a deep sense of belonging to their local history. It defines them and who they will be. Grandparents taught their grandchildren their town and family history and wanted their grandchildren to live up to their potential based on that history, be proud of it and come back and build the community with their talents.

The names of my students were not given to them by chance. They were thoughtful, meaningful, historic, predictive, and foreordained. They were names that would help them see and live up to their potential. The parents did not name them to be different. The naming process in China comes from historical meanings and cultures, and parents' desire for their children to become great in a particular type of character. Chinese children's names are given in the hopes that they will be inspired to live up to their names.

As we chatted in my room I discovered my students' real names, not their chosen American names. It was inspiring for me to hear them and see how they are living up to *the names given them*. The first name in Chinese is their family name, or for Americans their last name. The second name is their first. I would like to share some of my student's names and their meanings.

Yang is a first name meaning ocean. Her parents hoped she could accommodate hundreds of rivers like an ocean. Her interpretation is that she can gain a lot of knowledge and learn to be tolerant. She is the one student that showed up at my class every night. Her English was not the best, but she was determined to learn. As a result her English improved drastically and so did her knowledge.

Hong means rainbow, Yao means beautiful stone. Her father named her Hongyao hoping she would be a pretty stone shining on the rainbow during her lifetime. This young lady is a ray of sunshine and certainly lived up to her name. Her light is brilliant, colorful, and full of passion and love for others.

Hai means sea, Lian means lotus plant. Hailian's interpretation of her name means to have a broad and big heart and be beautiful. She indeed has a very big heart and welcomed me with open arms before classes even started. This student is shy and yet brave. As I walked across campus my first few days she approached me timidly and said hello. She was the first student I met and gave me such warmth in her smile and introduction I could hardly wait to meet the rest of my students.

Dan Dan means the only one, unique. That is spot-on for this young woman. Her parents have great expectations for her and she is following through with those expectations. Her parents are depending on her to be there for them in their later years. She has been extremely helpful and loving to her mother in particular. She has a unique happy, energetic and determined personality that is infectious to be around.

Lisha means beautiful. Her grandmother wanted her to do things efficiently, fast, and yet remain beautiful. She did just that. She moves quickly when she does things and had (and still has) high goals. When we needed things done she would follow through with exactness and proficiency. Lisha is also very beautiful inside and out.

Xiaojing means quiet morning because she was born on a quiet morning. Maybe that's why she has calmness about her.

Shijing comes from a family generational name. Shi is a name from her family history. Jing is an unusual name used in Chinese classics meaning *a talented girl.* Her grandfather named her hoping she would be a talented and pretty girl both in appearance and heart. She is an unusually tall statuesque young woman. She practices yoga and has a concern for others beyond most. She's intrigued by how the mind works and makes us do what we do and looks for ways to use her mind to help others.

Ruihua is two names put together. Rui means be happy and auspicious. Hua means beautiful. She is not only a very happy, positive, beautiful young woman, but also a very helpful one. This student showed leadership skills in my class from the beginning and was a great asset in the Academy office.

Zengwei has her own thoughts on how her name was interpreted. Zeng means honest, to be sincere with people around her. Wei means trust. She said her name was more of a boy's name. Her thoughts are that her father wanted her to grow like a man and persevere and be brave. Not only is this student honest and trustworthy, but she showed an uncanny ability for organization and keeping things going in the office as well.

Min has the meaning of being smart and intelligent. She is a very smart student who is willing to change many things in the world around her. She has an amazing handle on the English language and communicates very clearly. This came from a determination she had at a young age. She wanted so badly to speak English she would speak her thoughts out loud whenever she was outside on the playground in grade school on her own.

Meng Di is a delightful young lady, Meng means dream and Di means inspire. She was named by her grandfather. His goal for her was to have a dream in life and always be inspired by others. She has set many big goals and dreams for herself and consequently she's been an inspiration to those around her. Her happy, bubbly spirit cannot be ignored when you are in her presence.

Youfeng's parents had a wonderful hope and expectation for her future. Her name means dragon or Phoenix. Her parents named her this hoping she would fly in the sky out of difficult times like a Phoenix being reborn from fire. She truly impressed me as an individual who is rising up out of the ashes of difficulty and poverty. She is brilliant and getting an education, even though her family has had very little. She wants to make a difference in the lives of others and is making a mark on the business community. When she first shared her name with the other women in my room that evening some of them smiled and said, "That means dragon." When she shared the meaning her parents had hoped for, the mood changed. It became a beautiful name to live up to that obviously held hope for a bright and clear future.

Predicting the Future

As you can see Chinese names are not only a name. A person's name represents their culture, heritage, and future. It is a symbol of one's family and self. Many people look for a wise family member to name their babies. Others go outside their family and find a wise person in their village to pick a name. When the students shared their names with me they were all proud of the meanings. They felt as though it gave them a prediction of who they would become.

After being on campus for a few weeks, I came to realize the American names the students bore were just something they read about in a book or saw in a movie. Often students would walk up to me on campus and ask if I would give them an English name. This seemed like such a big responsibility to me. I would look into their eyes and get a sense of who they were and give them a name.

One of the students decided to give me a Chinese name of my own. It is Ling Qi meaning smart cookie. I told them a lot about all the cookies I made so that probably had an influence on the naming process. One of my student's mothers became a good friend of mine despite the language barrier. The name she gave me was Haomei, meaning wonderful sister.

My American name is Joyce. I often thought people were singing about me when they sang REJOICE in songs. Because it is derivative of joyful, I have always felt I should live a happy life and bring joy to others. The stories we tell about our names and why we were named such can impact who we become.

I am grateful to be a joyful person and to have that be who I was named to be.

The Magic of Miracles
Chapter Seven

IMAGINATION

Miracles are the natural way of the Universe - our only job is to move our doubting minds out of the way.
— Jonathan Lockwood Huie —

A miracle took me to China! I knew the moment I heard about the program I was supposed to go and had no idea how that was going to happen. I consider myself a fairly optimistic person who believes I can have or create pretty much whatever I want. But when it came to China that belief had its boundaries. Thinking I could have what I want was always confined in a container of my ability to control it, manage it or see how it could happen.

Over the years, I have learned that is not how miracles take place. They occur in a world outside of my ability to make them happen. They emerge in the world of grace or the world of weird. Have you ever experienced a miracle and said, "Wow that was strange. I don't understand how that happened." My life has been filled with miracles that I failed to acknowledge, or even notice, because I was too busy looking for something wrong, figure it out, or find a way to make it happen again. There were even times when a miracle would take place and I would say things like "*I have no idea how that happened and I don't expect it to happen again, because if I do I might jinx it.*" As if to say that when good things happen to me, it's just a fluke. I would even go as far as to ask myself questions like, "*How did I deserve this miracle? I haven't worked hard enough *to earn it.*" Miracles are not earned or deserved, they are gifts and it's up to me whether or not to accept those gifts with gratitude.

The first time I went to China in September 2011 was a miracle! The second time I went was spring 2012. After leaving my heart with my beautiful students I kept receiving emails from them with questions and concerns. I became the Chinese *Dear Abby*. After each email query, they ended it with "I will see you in the spring at our graduation and Women's Symposium." Smiling at the thought I knew that was not possible within the boundaries of what I could imagine, because it didn't fit into my understanding of things. How could I ever afford to go back? Just for fun I checked the flights to China to see what it would cost. When I saw the price I shut down the possibility.

However, the thought of going back for graduation tugged at me and caused me a lot of anxiety, fogginess and sadness. But my mind, my checkbook, my way of making it happen just couldn't see how such a trip was even possible.

In early March I called Steve (my husband) at work and told him "I have to go back to China in May!"

His response surprised me when he said, "I know."

"What?" I said. "If you knew why didn't you tell me?"

He replied, "I knew you would figure it out."

"But how am I supposed to pay for it? The prices on the flights are going up."

Steve is a believer in miracles and gave me the perfect response: "Put it on a credit card, the money will show up."

I hung up the phone shaking, smiling from ear to ear, hair rising on the back of my neck, my heart pounding, and I knew this is what I was supposed to do.

I have a good friend named Sherry with whom I shared all my experiences of growth after I returned from China. She was supportive and excited for my progression; she saw my growth and cheered me on. Sherry is a successful businesswoman, but stays in her own space. She works from home, her children all live within a few miles radius of her and she doesn't leave her house much. It is her preference. When I called Sherry to tell her I was going back to China you can imagine my surprise when she said "Well, damn it, get me a ticket, too, I'm going with you!" It was a miracle that Sherry was leaving her comfort zone. It shocked all her children, as well.

My next phone call was to Hannah, my daughter at college. When I told her I was going back for two weeks for a visit she shocked me, too. She said, "I have some money in savings, get me a ticket and I will go with you!" Oh, my goodness my life just turned upside down and inside out! The adrenal rush filled my whole body; I was shaking, full of excitement and fear. I immediately took action and booked three tickets to China! This is what I mean when I say, *Don't think about it, do what calls the minute you feel it.*

I felt like I was suddenly amped up on steroids. I answered the call inside me again, doing something hard, and yet it was exactly what I was supposed to do. As the time came closer for me to leave for China I was still waiting for the miracle to pay for my plane ticket. Four days before my departure a check came in the mail addressed to me. It was a payout from an investment Steve and I made ten years previous and it had never paid us anything. The check was in my name for the amount I needed for my trip! Steve smiled and said, "There you go, it's yours."

A miracle you might ask? Absolutely!

Sharing the Love

When the three of us arrived in China it was so much fun to watch and share all the loves I had for this country with Sherry and Hannah. I saw them turn up their noses at the smells, the dirt, the food, the smog, just like I had done on my first trip. But this time my reaction was just the opposite. None of that bothered me anymore, because it was China, a place in which I fell in love with the people, the land, the history and myself.

The students, on the other hand, fell in love with Hannah. After all, she was a peer from America, a new friend. She was very popular with my students, and the young men liked her, too.

One of our days there, we visited a home for handicapped children. (This is one of my favorite places to go. The kids there call me Nainai – grandma – and love the hugs and candy I freely hand out.) The teenage hearing-impaired kids were immediately drawn to Hannah. The way they communicated with her was by using paper and pen. They wrote down questions and my students would translate to Hannah and she would respond by asking her translators to write down her answers. As I watched her interaction with these students I started to cry. I saw my daughter embracing this new land, new environment and people with such love and kindness. One of the handicapped children came up from behind her and took a bracelet off her own arm and placed it on Hannah's wrist. Hannah hardly knew who put it there because there were so many students flocking around her. My daughter looked at me as I cried and a tear ran down her cheek, as well. "Mom, get those bracelets in my backpack I bought today to take home with me," she asked, still surrounded by her new fans.

As I handed her the bracelets she put them on each of the wrists of the students. It was a miracle moment for me to see the growth of my daughter, her love and compassion for those around her. I loved sharing my new passions and family with her, and then watch how quickly she fell in love with them.

Sherry was in awe of the kindness and service rendered to her by the student escorts. If there was anything she wanted or needed they were prepared to provide it. Even though the traffic shocked her, the food was not the most desirable, and everything was foreign to what she was used to at home, she quickly gained a love for the students and what they represented. In the end, that was all that mattered.

One day, some of our students took us to a local village well outside the city. We had to take two taxis to get us there. The girls were confident the village members would welcome us. When we arrived, my students stood at the front of the large red door of the first home we visited and called out things like, "We have friends from America that want to meet you."

As the big doors opened these kind people welcomed us into their courtyard and graciously offered us fruit from their trees. And of course, they asked us to stay for lunch. My guests loved how welcoming the people in the village were, even though we were complete strangers to them. Sherry was especially shocked at their friendly, accommodating offers. But I had grown accustomed to it.

Because we look so different from the locals, our presence in these villages usually brought people out of their homes, as if we were a parade to watch. When we were ready to leave the village our students headed toward a local bus stop. But a member of the community saw this and asked, "What are you doing? The busses will not be back today."

Once again, I did not worry. I thought the girls would figure it out and all would be okay. As it turns out, a motorcycle cart came by and one of my students waved him down. "Can you give us a ride (there were eight of us) to the closest city?

The driver agreed to do so for a fee, which we happily paid. Then we all crammed like sardines into the back of this little motorcycle-driven wagon. We resembled the occupants in a clown car at the circus. It was a great memory and a lot of fun.

Just Say Yes!

I went back to China because I realized I now have a big Chinese family! I knew I was supposed to be there. My first trip taught me that if I go with the flow great things will happen. When I returned, I saw my students' growth in the short seven months since I had been with them. The experience was all I could ever hope for and more, because I saw that my influence was not only helpful to them, but everlasting, as well. Teaching with confidence, sharing their dreams, witnessing miracles in their lives, moving through fears and doubts, letting them be the tool to growth was just a portion of what I observed.

When I returned to China I felt my whole worldview change for the better. When I came the first time, I saw my students begging for confidence. But now they boldly shared their voices and growth. I thought to myself, *they learn, and yet teach me, more than I will ever know! What a wonderful world!*

When it came time to go home from my second trip, the students asked, "When will you be back?"

I was honest. "I don't know, but I will be back." I knew it was not the end. I gave up thinking that I wouldn't return. That second trip taught me that anything is possible if I turn it over to the world of miracles.

And I did go back. I have been to China five times since I first learned about the Women's Academy. Each time miracles paid for me to get there. One time I asked for donations on Facebook (this was way out of my comfort zone). I stated "I am returning to China to teach, if anyone has an organization or business that would like to sponsor me I am open to donations." When I posted that statement I almost threw up, it was so against my nature. I wanted to take back the post, but I didn't have the computer knowledge to retrieve it.

Within a week of posting my call for donations I started receiving money in the mail anonymously; fifty-dollar bills, one-hundred dollar bills, all placed in envelopes addressed to me, but with no return address. Friends handed me cash. My nephew came over a few times and gave me whatever he had in his wallet, which balanced out to a few hundred dollars. My neighbors dropped off an envelope with a couple hundred dollars in it. A kind, elderly man from church called me one day and told me he wanted to give me some money. I stopped by his house and he handed me $300. He said, "If I had more I would give it to you." I was so grateful for the kindness and generosity of all those who helped. It was out of my reach, but I knew it was what I was supposed to do, so I let the miracles flow.

Airport Miracles

Each time I left China there was always a little glitch. Knowing it was coming, I became a little uneasy every time I had to leave. My fifth visit was the most alarming. On that trip, another friend of mine, Sharyn, went with me to teach and we had a wonderful time together. I purchased both of our tickets at the same time on a flight discount website. When we went to China there was no problem. But when we left China it was another story. At the airport, we approached the ticket counter with our confirmation numbers and itineraries. Customs stamped her passport and gave her a boarding pass. But when they looked at mine they started talking to me in Mandarin, pointing to the ticket and shaking their heads no. One of our students (who had come along to walk us through the process) tried to help, but had no idea what to do. As I stood there wondering what would happen next Grace (a previous student from a year earlier) showed up to see me off at the airport. She listened and argued with the ticket lady, then ran with my ticket to the main desk. My friend and I followed. I had no idea what to do. I told Sharyn, "Get on your flight, you have a ticket that works, I will catch up with you on our layover in Beijing." I did a lot of praying and hoped things would work out for me to go home without having to buy a new ticket.

After about an hour Grace came over and said, "They say your ticket has been cancelled and that you must buy a new one."

I asked her, "Can you get me on a fast train to Beijing?"

"Of course," she said. "But we will have to take the bus to the train station."

As Grace and I sat on the bus I looked out the window and thought *This would be a good time for a miracle.* At that moment, I realized I already had my miracle. It was Grace. She showed up, walked me through the steps and got me on the train. But now my concern was how would I get through the train station with three pieces of luggage up and down stairs?

There were no elevators. Grace turned to me and said, "I will accompany you to Beijing. I want to make sure you make it to your plane safely."

I started to cry and replied sincerely, "Grace you are my guardian angel. You have helped me so much and have answered my question of how I will I manage getting myself to Beijing."

When we got to the train station Grace dropped me off at a little restaurant and said, "Get something to eat and I will go buy the tickets."

I bought us both lunch and waited. It was a holiday weekend and very crowded.

When she returned she said, "You won't believe this, but I bought the last two tickets to Beijing. There was only one left on the regular train so I got you one first class. I will drop you off in your train car and then I'll go to mine." Can you imagine my depth of gratitude for this sweet angel? I overflowed with appreciation and the miracles that unfolded in a three-hour time frame.

When we got on the train I sat down, got settled and Grace went to her train car. It was then I received a text from a good friend in Ghana. Her name is Patience. She is the strongest woman of faith I have ever met. We only talk about five or six times a year. She didn't know where I was, but her text said this: "My dear sister, I hope you are well. I was just thinking of you and feeling such love for you and your family. All is well with me. I pray you will be blessed with a peaceful mind, Love Patience." How on earth did she know I needed a peaceful mind at that moment in time? I immediately texted her back saying, "Thank you for being so in tune to your heart that you know what I need. Yes, I could use your prayers and belief that I will get on my plane back home."

I had guardian angels all around me.

Grace got me through the maze of taxi drivers and masses of people at the train station in Beijing. Everyone saw an American and wanted to charge me a bundle to get to my hotel. She pushed them aside and called a cab to pick us up on the curb for a quarter of the price everyone else was charging.

Another one of my past students, Mandy, worked in Beijing. She had made the arrangements for my hotel, as well as a visit to the Great Wall of China the following day before we flew home. She picked up Sharyn at the airport and then took her shopping and to dinner. I told Mandy, "I won't be able to go to the Great Wall because I need to get to the airport early to make sure I have a ticket home."

Her response was, "I have already been to the airport and everything is okay with your ticket, you are safe to go now."

Through my tears, I hugged and thanked her profusely. She and Grace got me through a frightening experience and yet I never thought *I won't get home*. I knew it would all work out.

I wasn't there to lose faith. I was there because I knew that was where I was supposed to be. I was taken care of all the way and miracle after miracle took place, which reminded me that I was not in charge of this experience. I was on it for the ride and growth.

Letting go of being in charge was a new experience for me. Believing and accepting miracles was one of the best ways I learned to let go.

Enjoying cookies on my first day in China.

Judi and me in the fall of 2011.

Sias campus located in Zingheng China.

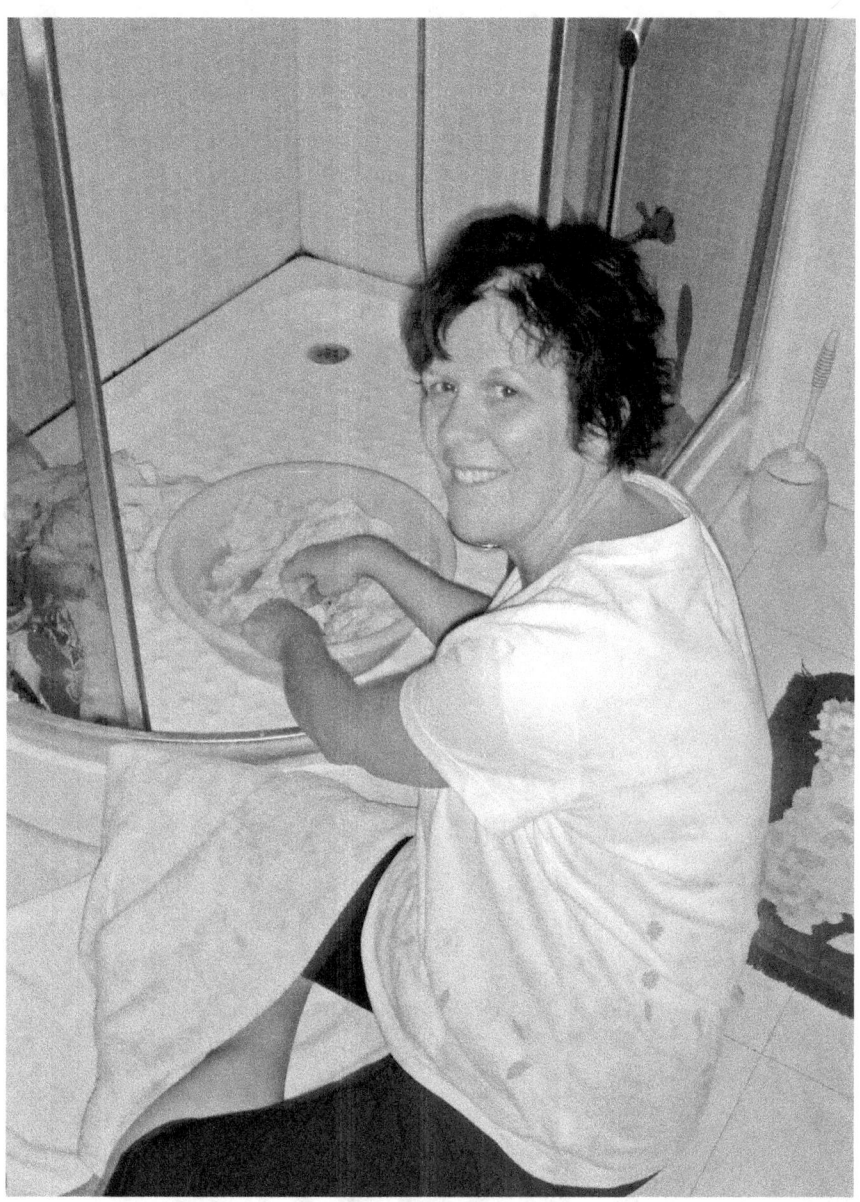

Doing laundry in the shower of my dorm room.

My classroom at The World Academy for Women.

Enjoying a rooftop dance party with my students.

Getting around town.

My favorite street food – baked crackers.

Enjoying a traditional meal in a Chinese restaurant.

Grace's mother and me during a visit to Grace's village.

Graduation day with some of my students.

A typical Chinese village home.

At The Great Wall with Sharyn and Grace.

In a pomegranate orchard with our tour guide and the orchard owner.

Grace and Gloria with me in Phoenix for a visit.

Dan Dan and I shopping while she was in Phoenix to visit.

One of Selia's visits to Phoenix.

My husband Steve and me with Susanna when she came to Phoenix to visit.

Transmit the Love
Chapter Eight

GRATITUDE

Gratitude makes sense of our past, brings peace for today, and creates a vision for tomorrow.
— Melody Beattie —

I opened my heart in China without even realizing it. My students loved me like a bee to the flower, they came for the nectar and I was able to provide it. They wanted more light, passion, vision, and possibilities so they could reach higher levels of their true selves. What I shared and taught extended them beyond their personal histories and limitations from the past. In turn, I was able to step out of my own blocks, fears, limitations and lack of faith from my past.

Gratitude for what I experienced is such a small word. There must be a grander explanation for what I felt. A Chinese proverb says, "A bit of fragrance clings to the hand that gives flowers." For everything I gave I received so much more. The beauty of sharing and teaching those who wanted what I had to give brought out my own magnificence and the ability to acknowledge it. Not only did I receive gratitude, I lived, breathed and spoke my gratitude daily. For nearly a week before I left, my students showed up at my door and in class with gifts, tokens of their love and thankfulness. They wanted so desperately to make sure I knew how much they appreciated me. They could not afford to buy things, but they delivered gifts anyway. I received many notes, and emails of gratitude for what I taught while I was there. It was beyond anything I had ever experienced.

One afternoon I sat in the audience of a large auditorium with the women of the Academy listening to a speaker. Someone passed me a note that said, "Joyce, do you see the beautiful sunflowers on the stage? You must know your beauty surpasses any beauty of these flowers." Where on earth did such a note come from, and totally unsolicited? As I turned around to see who it may have come from I saw one of my students waving to me, I held up the note with a question on my face and she nodded.

After teaching for three weeks (on my initial trip), things started looking different to me. I put on a different pair of glasses. Suddenly, the smells, the food, the dirt, the inconveniences all became a thing of the past. My morning walks brought me so much joy to see the beauty of the campus and the students studying and practicing what they learned. I came across a young man one morning on my walk who decided to join me so he could practice his English. To my surprise he had an English accent. When I asked him about it he said, "I am practicing my English accent by watching BBC on the Internet. I want to speak like an Englishman."

I simply smiled and said, "I think your English is great and your accent is delightful. Good luck, I would be happy to have you practice with me anytime."

I enjoyed my walks along the river next to campus because it brought me out into the culture of the land. Many times I would pass local fisherman squatting next to the water with their pointed hats, bamboo fishing poles, smoking and listening to their transistor radio. I wanted to strike up a conversation with them about the catch of the day, but did not have the language skills to do so. I simply smiled and enjoyed the music. Yes, I enjoyed the music. Originally when I first heard the twangs and tunes of Chinese music it hurt my ears. Now it brought me joy and peace. All along the river were little areas fenced off with bamboo sticks and string, setting the boundary of a vegetable garden. I only imagined (but had no real confirmation) that these spaces were pieces of land that locals gratefully found to use for personal planting. It impressed me how they utilized whatever ground they could find to grow food. They were very industrious from my viewpoint. It made me feel grateful for my own home, yard, and garden.

Giving Back

I had the awesome and challenging opportunity to be on a committee for deciding who would receive a need-based scholarship at the Women's Academy. Numerous students applied and were narrowed down to six by another committee who read their applications. Each of the six student applicants came before a committee of five Americans (I was one of them) in a large boardroom on campus and shared their story and the reason for needing the scholarship. It was a painful experience to hear of their hardships in their personal lives and families. All of them sweat bullets during their presentations, shaking and crying, mostly because they had to speak English in front of five foreigners. It took all I had to not go over and hug every one of them and say, "It's okay, we are just human beings here with our own problems listening to what you have to tell us." I tried my best to encourage them and make them feel comfortable. This scholarship was what would keep them in school so it was very important.

The decision regarding who had the greatest need was a hard one. If I had the money I would have given them each a scholarship. After discussing with the other committee members, we unanimously chose a young girl who was studying accounting. Her family life was experiencing extreme difficulty with illness, high medical costs, and loss of jobs. Nevertheless, she set wonderful goals to receive an education and get a good job to support her immediate and extended family members. When she received notice that the scholarship was awarded to her she was so grateful she sent a letter of gratitude to all the committee members and the donor of the scholarship.

The following is an excerpt from her five-page gratitude letter:

"I owe you my best thanks! You help me to get out of the trouble. I'm very much obliged to you! I cherish the opportunity very much. The aid has lightened the burden of my family. I'll study harder and take more socially useful activities. It's essential for me to help the students who have troubles around me warmly. I'll transmit the love."

Her last sentence, *I'll transmit the love*, is her way of saying *I'll pass it on*, or *pay it forward*. I fell in love with those words.

Pay It Forward

Upon my return home after that first trip, my thoughts were much the same: *I'll transmit love*. I was beyond appreciative for my experience. I had been given a new set of wings to fly. How will I transmit the love? The experience I'd just had was a miracle that I wanted to pass on to someone else.

When I came back to the same situation (an empty house) that I had left when I ran to China, I felt different. Now I had this compelling passion to do something more, to offer personal transformation to others like I had experienced. Sure, my incompetence and inadequacies showed up, but I had something to give and my voice was meant to be heard. I didn't need the praise of others to affirm my self-worth. My cumulated experiences felt like a bubbling volcano inside of me waiting to erupt so I could share all I had learned.

Gratitude in all things helped me through my adjustment when I came home. Of course, all the modern conveniences and comforts of home were wonderful after living without them. I have never been so grateful for being born in the United States with so many privileges. I think for the first time I was thankful to be me. As I looked in the mirror of my vanity I liked who I saw. It wasn't the outer appearance that I found attractive; it was what was inside, that *thing* that now shone through my eyes. *Maybe*, I thought, *this is what the students saw, the glow, the yearning, love, inspiration, confidence, and passion*. It *was* me. I realized no matter who I was or where I came from I had been given this amazing opportunity to wake up and share my gifts. I was making an impact on myself and on other women in a small rural town in China.

The first commitment I made when I returned home was to say "Yes" to whatever I was asked to do, especially if it was out of my comfort zone. That was my expression of gratitude and true self. A voice spoke to my heart when I asked God, *"Now what am I to do?"* The answer was, *"Teach what you learned."* I had no idea where I was supposed to teach but I was ready and watching for the door of opportunity to open.

Within two weeks of my return from China, and making that commitment, numerous organizations asked me to speak. I spoke in front of church groups, businesses, women's organizations and at the local community college. I jumped at those opportunities because I loved sharing my stories. After a short five weeks, China had become my second home, and the women in the Academy were part of my family. On a regular basis, I spoke at least twice a month for a whole year. Once I was in the flow of saying *yes* to new experiences the opportunities showed up. I also had to say *no* to ones that didn't coincide with the direction I was headed.

Public speaking became something I love. Every story I told brought me right back to my China home and I was able to cement that feeling even deeper in my heart. My confidence didn't stem from being looked up to or admired, it was a direct result of doing the things that pushed and challenged me. I felt like a new person every time I spoke to an audience. It was fun to see where I had been and how far I had come.

China was the beginning of my metamorphous, it was not the end. I didn't know I was in the chrysalis when I embarked on my first trip, but as it started to open, and the world took on new meaning and purpose, I began to spread my wings. I got a glimpse of my true self and it was up to me what I did with it. I don't know if it would have been possible to see and experience that without walking blindly into the unknown. After I returned home, I was so motivated to stay on the path I started while in China, to see where I could fly. I couldn't be stopped. I wanted more.

But "more" meant I had to keep moving into uncharted territory.

I Am Amazing
Chapter Nine

APPRECIATION

*At the center of your being you have the answer,
you know who you are and you know what you want.*
— Lao Tzu —

"**Is it really okay to say I am amazing?**" Those were the words that came out of my mouth one night in China when I Skyped with my husband after class.

He was excited to hear me say such a thing, especially since I had been so down and out just a mere few days before. And now it was obvious that my exuberance and joy overflowed and could not be contained. He said to me. "You have to blog about this right now while you're completely present to it."

I was a little taken aback. "I can't say I'm amazing," I replied. "It sounds vain and boastful. I am embarrassed to say it out loud and even more embarrassed to write it." How could I say such a thing and put it where people would see it?

But fortunately I got over that and wrote the blog post "I Am Amazing," anyway. I posted it one evening, and afterward I was shocked and almost ashamed of myself. When I awoke the next morning I questioned what I had done. *Can I handle it when other people like themselves and speak well about who they are?* The answer is *yes* and *no*. It depends on how they do it and if they sound boastful or just confident.

I, on the other hand, couldn't seem to handle it either way. I taught confidence to these young women, and felt it myself, and liked the feeling, but I couldn't seem to acknowledge and accept it. I found myself afraid to admit to others that I felt confident for fear they would be uncomfortable around me. However, I kept thinking about that Maryanne Williamson quote: "There is nothing enlightened about shrinking so that people won't feel insecure around you." *What was I doing?* I thought. I wanted to be confident and teach confidence, but shrink while doing it? That did not make sense. It was not part of the game plan and I would not let myself be that way.

When I developed my curriculum and PowerPoint presentation before I left for China I felt secure in knowing I would have something to refer to while I taught. But when I walked into that classroom ready to teach, I didn't experience what I thought would happen. When I stood in front of my students it felt as though I became someone else. I was not the person I knew. It was like someone else emerged from my deep knowingness. She came from a source I had never accessed before or at least didn't recognize.

Guess what happened when I was far away from anyone I knew, or who knew me? I was forced to find my own inner strength. I didn't have anyone else to defer to, fall back on or catch the slack. It was me and whatever helpers, guides or higher power from which I could get instruction. I was pleasantly surprised and very grateful to see what I could accomplish without another human being backing me up. I knew I had help from above. But I did not know I had it in me all along. I thought this kind of confidence and awareness only happened in the movies or for other people. It was not only empowering but a confidence-builder like no other. There was something about feeling like a conduit for greater things in other people that was such a miracle for me. The fact that I was willing to do what was scary (move out of my comfort zone and listen to my heart) is the thing that made it possible.

I started to wonder, *"Has this been in me the whole time? Was I so busy trying to be someone else that I wasn't open to seeing it?"* This beautiful version of myself was never visible to me because I couldn't allow myself to be that vulnerable. Everything was a competition for me, but all I ended up doing was compare my worst to everyone else's best. It was refreshing and invigorating to feel like I had something wonderful in me to contribute and share that made a difference in the lives of others.

I found myself teaching curriculum that was inspiring, meaningful and powerful. It was exhilarating and fun just to let the words and lessons flow out of my mouth. The stories from my life's experiences were metaphors that applied to the topics I taught. Each time one ended, the students would say "Tell us another story."

The Confidence Experiment

When I taught the women, I encouraged them to exhibit confidence by owning up to who they were, and believe what they had to offer was of value. I also asked them to think of something hard they wanted to do, but was afraid to admit, and then do it. That is where confidence is found, not in a book, nor can it really be taught. My experience of being in China is what built my confidence because I did it, and it was hard. Doing something challenging is where you find confidence. I not only instructed my students, but spoke to my inner self, as well. I did believe in what I was teaching and knew it had great value. The proof was in my students. I could see the changes in them and how they lived their lives.

Similarly, there were changes in *me* and how I *lived my life*, as well. *This is good stuff*, I thought. *What if I like myself? Is that possible? Could I really like me just the way I am? What would it take for me to acknowledge my strengths and really shine?*

In one of the classes I helped the students write their speeches about the projects they had been working on. One of the group projects was to raise money to send to village children for school lunches by holding fundraisers. I asked them: "What would it be like for you to sit at lunch with an empty plate when the people around you were eating?" I could tell this really resonated with my class. "To grab your audience," I continued, "put an empty plate in front of one member of the audience and a full one in front of the other. Ask which plate do they want to be theirs? Then ask for donations to fill the plates of the students who had nothing." My thoughts turned briefly to my empty plate (which was my childless home) and how the women of the Academy had filled my plate with what I hungered for and I was filling theirs. That evening I wrote in my journal, "My cup runneth over with love."

I told my students, "I hope you are all taking notes, because this is good information and I don't know if I can pull it out of myself again." The students' little hands flew across their notebooks, writing down everything. One of them asked, "I love what you are saying, can you please speak a little slower?"

I chuckled and realized I talk way too fast when I am excited. Obviously, they had a language barrier to deal with that I didn't take into consideration. Speaking slowly became a constant awareness for me after that because I wanted them to get everything I said.

I had become a conduit in teaching these students. All I knew was that when I taught I accessed the parts of myself I didn't know existed! After all these years, China is where I found my true self, the part of me that loved people, and loved teaching. For the first time, I trusted my knowingness, my heart, and I let it guide me. I felt free from the constraints of self-judgment and comparisons, because there were none. I was just me, the me I hadn't met before. I was more whole than ever before. My *knowingness* instinctively knew that I didn't know the real me when I jumped at the opportunity to go to China. But once I got there, all my fears dissipated, because my confidence grew daily.

It was the audience that made my transformation possible, I thought to myself. They were so eager to learn and hear what I had to say. It was as though I had candy falling out of my mouth and they gobbled it up like hungry children. It was so rewarding to teach students that didn't want me to stop. In the United States students typically pack up their belongings ten minutes before class ends. But not these students, they moaned when I told them class ended at nine in the evening. The authentic feeling that I was *really* helping someone who wanted more was amazing. It nearly took my breath away each time it happened. Every class I taught I wondered, *Will this happen again?* It did because I was open to it and to being a vessel. I had such gratitude for the opportunity to be of service in that way. I realized it is what brought me there and that it was meant to be.

I thought, *How could I teach this or pass on the experiences I'd had?* True, maybe not everyone is as lost as I was or searching for new ways of being. I'm sure there are a lot of people who are content to stay right where they are. Obviously, they don't need me, and that's fine. I decided I had to find those who wanted to experience change, find purpose and passion. Those are the people who need me. That's who I would teach.

It is possible, if one is willing or in enough pain like I was, to make a choice to walk into the unknown to find what you're looking for. It is not something that can be bottled up and sold. It has to be experienced, and can't be found in a book or a Youtube video. Like I did, YOU must make an individual choice to walk into the unfamiliar places, take risks, be vulnerable and uncomfortable and find your personal change for yourself.

I knew when I agreed to go to China I could not back out. If I did I would have been left in a pool of depression. I also knew that after I made the commitment to teach, these women expected me to show up. The tug at my heart would not let go, it just kept pulling. I had to move past the chatter in my brain that said I couldn't do it. *You're not qualified. It's frightening. It's out of the norm for me.* Yes, I was afraid, very afraid and had a lot to learn. But the fear of who I would become if I didn't go was worse than going. Even though my safe place was where I felt miserable, it was what I knew. It was the unknown that scared me and yet that is where I met myself. What I have learned since then is that the unknown, the uncontrolled outcome and discomfort, is exactly where you make the biggest and most profound discoveries.

When China called to my heart and brought me out of my comfort zone I stepped into a very unfamiliar land, culture and territory. Yet when I did it, I felt ALIVE! I discovered parts of me I had never seen before. The moment I said, "I am amazing," I believed it with all my heart, because I knew it was not only me saying it. The revelation was bigger than me. I had help and guides that directed my experience, the hand of a greater power moved me through each step. It's as though doors opened the minute I said, "Yes."

And they never stopped opening after that.

What's Possible?

Anything was possible once I surrendered my will and what and how I wanted things to be. It took a great deal of trust to be so far away from home and just let things happen. After acknowledging that I am amazing, I never looked back. I wanted to be available for all the miracles that were awaiting me while I was there.

I said "YES" to everything I was asked to teach while I was in China. All the *"No's"* became irrelevant because I gave my word and followed through. For example, another university nearby asked me to come to their Psychology department and teach a graduate class. This scared the heck out of me. I hired a driver and took one of my students with me to translate. When I arrived, they introduced me to the head of the department who asked me to instruct them on using their new biofeedback equipment; a whole new wing in the building was dedicated to biofeedback. I didn't have a clue how to help them, but I agreed to be a test subject as they experimented using the machines.

One of the biofeedback machines was a nice relaxing massage chair. I sat in it and they clipped a probe to my pointer finger. Next to the chair was a computer screen with a dismal black and white picture of a dead forest. While eight Chinese professors stood over me and watched, they instructed me to relax and make the forest bloom. I had no idea how that was going to happen. I asked myself, *"What on earth do I think I am doing?*

And how am I going to relax while these professors stare at me?" I closed my eyes and thought of my grandchildren running in my front door (I missed them so much) calling my name, "Mammie, Mammie" (that is what they call me) and jumping into my open arms with their hugs and kisses. As I lay there in the chair with this pleasant memory tears ran down my cheeks into my hair, dropping into my ears. I couldn't wipe them because my finger was connected to the probe. I was concerned the professors would wonder why I was crying. Then suddenly I was brought back to the present with the *oohs* and *ahs* from the professors. I opened my eyes and to my astonishment the dismal forest was in full bloom and had a rainbow across the screen. *Wow, I thought, look at what my mind can do. I wondered, What else can I do with this powerful mind of mine? It was awesome to see that the power of my thoughts could change the picture on the screen. In that moment I wanted to change all my thoughts and make my life a picture in full bloom.*

It was so easy in China to see my amazing self for various reasons and for no reason at all. I could see so many outstanding, admirable, brilliant qualities in my students that they couldn't see in themselves. I had to point it out to them. I realized in that moment, if I can see that in them, I have a blueprint of the same in me. I couldn't see it in others if I didn't have some of it in myself. That thought was what changed me when I got home. I knew if I could see the greatness in others then I had greatness in me, as well.

Since then, I have never been the same.

Who Defines Me?
Chapter Ten

TRUTH

*Can you remember who you were
before the world told you who you should be?*
— Danielle La Porte —

I grew up in a home in which I struggled to have my own identity. The real me was always defined by my circumstances and how others saw me. I bought into every nickname and label given to me. I was the baby, the youngest child of six; the "baby" label worked for me when I didn't want to do something. I didn't know how to distinguish or separate who I was from my brother and sisters. I refused to see my true self whatever that was. I didn't even believe there was such a thing. If someone asked me, "Who are you?" my response was "Evan's sister, Joyce, the baby of the family," or "Mom's helper," or "My big sister's little sister."

But when I finally got glimpses of my true self as I got older, she was pretty powerful and had a lot to say. Honestly, it scared me. What if I expressed myself the way *she* wanted? I might get rejected, punished, or ignored. It was safer to fit in and blend, take on what others said. If someone complimented me on something, I was that *thing*. "You are so kind and fun," meant I was kind and fun. If someone ridiculed me, I took that on, as well. If someone told me, "You're so stupid. You don't know how to do that," I believed what they said and took it on as part of my identity. I spent most of my adolescent years believing I was dumb, because I grabbed that label and then played dumb. It took a good friend in college and a bet we made to test my intelligence. When I got my first 4.0 I was shocked and realized I had bought into a label that didn't belong to me.

Sometimes words didn't even have to be said. I had such a strong need to please others and be liked that I refused to be anything other than what other people projected onto me. It seemed so easy to take on others' views of me. I had a lot of fear of being rejected, not loved and alone. That fear drove me to please others so I would never be alone.

All this is hard for me to admit now, because it is not how people see me today. In fact, it feels quite vulnerable to be this honest. I have always been involved in volunteer projects in the community, church, and school. I was a leader and spoke to groups often, but behind all that I had a feeling of incompetence and inadequacy. Those with whom I have worked would say they saw me as confident and a *get-it-done* kind of person.

I do know how to get things done, but I have not always felt confident in doing so. I was a great pretender. I got things done so I wouldn't be judged. That's why I was afraid to fail. When asked on an application what my strengths are, I always wrote, "I like people and they like me." That is something I don't pretend. I really do like people. I knew (and still know now) how to be with people. I have good social skills. I don't have the gift of music, art or sports, but I do have the gift of making others feel comfortable. Growing up with a father who was a salesman and teaching me to sell products door to door by the age of eight put me at ease with humans. No one was a stranger to me. In fact, I love talking to strangers and hearing their stories.

Don't get me wrong, I wasn't a complete wet rag back then. I have a very rebellious side, too. I don't like being told what to do. I fight back and get stubborn when someone demands I do something I don't agree with. Maybe that's why I looked confident before I went to China. But even so, when it came to who I was (my ego and my identity) I let others define me. I was afraid to look anywhere else. What if I didn't like what

I found? What if I expressed my thoughts honestly? Would others turn away from me?

It was too risky to find out.

My Heritage

Your past inescapably defines your future if you don't know how to reconcile with it. As a child, I had experiences in life that were not always happy. I grew up with some discomforts and violence. But this does not have to define my identity today. For years I allowed it to be so until it became a story that I needed to be complete. However, it simply was what it was, an experience. I had to give up the lies I had been told and claim the truth I knew and felt about myself. Unfortunately this truth did not always show itself (or if it did I refused to acknowledge it) and I would inevitably fall back and believe the lies. It seemed easier to believe the lies over the truth, because the lies were familiar. They are what I heard for many years, so I accepted them.

I was born to be my brother's playmate and was told that from an early age. So that is exactly who I believed I was and I lived up to that identity to its full potential. My brother and I had many wonderful years playing together and being each other's buddy throughout childhood and adolescence. He is two years older than me and is my hero. I never wanted to disappoint him. Therefore, whatever he told me about myself I believed. Whatever he liked, I liked, whatever he felt, I felt. I was enmeshed with him. I could not acknowledge anything I saw differently for fear he would reject me.

My mother gave me a lot of positive feedback by complimenting me on anything I did. Her words fed my confidence. I liked believing what she said, it was encouraging and affirming. She told me I was creative, a good cook, and generous. My father tried to compliment me, too. But when he told me I did something good , he followed it up with, "But you could've done it differently." I only heard everything after the "but" and felt like I couldn't measure up. My father was usually quite critical of me, so I believed the criticism.

I spent most of my life looking to others to measure up. I tried to see whose life appeared happy and what they were doing so I could do that, too. *How can I live like the person I compared myself to?* It made for a difficult life because I always compared myself to the most awesome, beautiful, accomplished, high achievers. As a result, I never measured up. Instead, my good intentions created jealousy and competition, all of which created a constant battle.

I married a brilliant, kind man whom I loved and worshipped. It took many years for me to realize that he, too, had imperfections (just like everyone) and that I needed to stop competing with him. It is not healthy, nor does it lead to a loving relationship to constantly measure myself against my spouse.

My True Self

While in China I did not compare myself or compete with anyone. I did not worry about how anyone saw or experienced me. I didn't have anyone to hide behind or have to pretend to be anything other than who I was. The students owned me with their love. They were so full of generosity. Upon my arrival in China I immediately experienced an outpouring of gratitude, appreciation and service from each of my students. They were childlike in their love and light. They did not know anything about me. I had no past, only the present to live into. It was as though I was given a clean canvas on which I could paint anything I wanted.

Even though we can find ourselves through others, that is not the only place to look for our identity. Too often I pursued others' opinions to affirm my own self-worth, *but only if it was negative.* On the other hand, when my students shared an appreciation that resonated inside and spoke to my heart, I accepted it. I did not turn it away. Too many times in my life when someone shared a compliment I would deny it or flat out not believe it.

The other thing that gave me a glimpse into my true self was being vulnerable and open to hear the good, powerful, honest sharing of thoughts and feelings by my students. There was no fear, I didn't have to defend myself or be someone I wasn't in order for them to be honest with me. I believed what they said, whether it was about me or not. Having an open heart revealed a whole new perspective to see who I am.

My true self resonates from my experiences and how I see myself. When I became a conduit of knowledge for the women at the Academy, words came out of my mouth without self-judgement, fear or hesitation. Why? Because my ego and identity were no longer my driving force. Instead it was my true self lighting the way. I didn't own what was coming out of my mouth as me. I was simply a vessel to teach from my heart.

You might ask, "What *is* your true self?" There are a lot of self-help books, groups, and gurus who teach about finding one's true, divine self. Fortunately for me, I found it without reading a book, but rather by experiencing it firsthand. You can find yours too, by doing the unthinkable, the thing your heart has been telling you to do for a long time, but you've been too afraid to do it. What is it you are afraid to say or even admit that you want to do? Books are great, but experience is where the rubber meets the road, where you will witness yourself in ways you never imagined. It took me stepping into uncertain realms to find myself. This is where my foundation for confidence was built. Doing hard things is what gave me the courage to do more hard things.

Before I went to China I did not see myself as anything more than mediocre. It didn't take more than teaching two classes for me to feel like a rock star. Not only did the fame come from my students' responses, but it also came from within *me*. I started to feel differently about myself because I saw who I truly was. Inevitably after every class someone wanted to take a picture with me. Out in public, people often handed their babies to me and asked to take my picture with their child. One afternoon while walking down a busy city street, a teenager approached giggling and asked to take a picture with me. After that all her friends wanted one, as well. This may have made me feel important in the past. It was a common thing for most Americans to have their picture taken and it was not what gave me confidence or built me up. It wasn't things, people or compliments that made me like myself. *How I felt* about myself was all that mattered. I learned that all definitions of who I am from any other source, other than my heart and higher power, are simply not true.

I claimed my truth in China.

Can I Keep This Up?

When I returned to the states I slowly fell back into the mode of being concerned about how others saw me. It took constant effort and presence to stay in my own life and out of the lives of others, to not worry about what they thought of me or what they were doing. I recognized the difference right away. My feelings of inadequacy kept me from being focused and doing what I wanted to do. This was a distraction. I had trouble sustaining the great feelings I had about myself when I was in China. But that only meant I had to dig a deeper foundation that I could take with me anywhere. Sometimes it took saying the words out loud, "Is this really who I want to be?" Other times it took recognizing the good I was doing, so I could stop comparing myself to others. I have words I say to myself when I start my comparisons: "I am grateful for my gifts and qualities and for the gifts of others. I appreciate the wonderfulness and uniqueness in myself, as well as that of each human being I meet." I even placed these statements on my vison board so I would read them daily. Another one is "I experience joy every day and spark joy in others, and I celebrate the radiance in myself and others." These words keep me focused on who I am and how I can share with those around me.

When I stay out of others' lives and let them have their own experiences, I am clearer on who I am, because their lives are theirs and mine is mine. I am more aware of each step I take, every breath, moment and feeling I have. It is very freeing to just live my life, and not that of my kids, my husband, my siblings, and my friends. I enjoy taking part in the lives of those I love, but I do not have to live in their shoes and fit in to be me.

The awareness of "I am not alone, I have help from beyond me" became more prevalent each day. The realization that I am uniquely me, nobody is me, or like me, and never will be, is a powerful awareness. So I asked myself, "Why should I compare?" An awareness I had about comparisons came when I realized it's okay if life challenges me to be a better person. That's it. If my competition is to put someone else down then it's not in harmony with who I want to be. No matter who I am or where I come from I am part of a bigger picture and I allow myself to step into that.

The fog broke in China. I became elevated enough to see the full landscape. I made an impact on the lives of women there and they made an equally large impression on me. If I had played small as their teacher, I would have never seen this part of me. It wasn't just in China that I had to take those leaps. It has to happen everywhere in my life, regardless of where I am. What I saw and learned in China was the catalyst to bigger things and that experience left me with the confidence I need to continue taking those leaps. I started a self-excavation while I was there without even knowing what I was doing, which generated unbelievable personal growth.

And now the treasures just keep revealing themselves.

What's Next?
Chapter Eleven

ENJOY

Life is about not knowing, having to change, taking the moment and making the best of it without knowing what's going to happen next.
— Gilda Radner —

I like the coasting sensation when going down a hill on a bike, the smooth sailing on calm waters, or the soft sway of a swing in the breeze. Staying where it is comfortable is a motto from my past. Every time I hike with my husband and kids I seldom go to the top with the rest of them. I am one who reaches a point, sits and says, "I'm done. I will enjoy the view from here and wait for you." I would rather sit under a tree and meditate or put my feet in the stream than go further if I am content with my current view. Since my China experience, I have definitely seen changes in my usual or past behavior that is contrary to being content and stopping.

After my return from China I was hiking in Yosemite Park with my husband and noticed there were two trail options to reach a scenic lake. One trail was paved and the other was rocky and steep. We chose the rocky path. I was surprised with my decision to choose the more difficult one without hesitation. But the rocky one looked more scenic and that is what I wanted. As we hiked the rugged terrain I was very present to each step I took because there were large rocks in the path and I did not want to stumble. I would take a few steps, glance down to be cautious, then stop and gaze up at the massive granite walls around me. The view was spectacular when I looked up. I had to look down to watch my step but did not hesitate to pause and take in the panoramic view. If I had to climb over a large boulder it made me stop and look at the land around me the trees, and foliage on the ground. I moved slowly which made me see more and take in what was around me completely. It actually reminded me of my steps in China. I was very cautious there and watched where I walked and stepped on the marble stairs and walkways that wove throughout campus. Because of my intentional steps I saw more and recognized the detail of things.

I Am Not Who I Was

I continue to be amazed at the changes in myself after going to China. I chose to do something that was hard and it opened my eyes to so much personal growth. Once I saw the expanded vision of who I am, I wanted to increase the view. Some people look at my life and say, "Wow, you have it so good, you are so lucky." I heard that a lot in China from my students. It is true, I do (and did) have it good and have been truly blessed in many ways. I also find I get stagnate and forego any expansion of myself if I stay in the security of what I know, of having it so *good*.

One afternoon I had lunch with a friend I have known for a long time. When I shared with her how I saw myself before I went to China versus how I see myself now she was shocked. She couldn't believe I really felt that way about myself, then or now. Her statement to me was, "I think you are the bravest person I know."

I literally laughed out loud at that statement and said, "You're kidding. Why? Do you think I am brave because I went to China? Or because I say yes to things that scare me?"

She responded, "Because you do things I wouldn't do."

I realized then, *Maybe I have more courage than I give myself credit for.*

Forging Ahead

After returning home from China I did not let myself coast into oblivion and bask in the wonderful things I learned. I forced myself not to lay low. Part of me wanted to do nothing, but I knew better. Because it was so empowering to see what I saw in myself, I wanted to see what I could do to continue the path I started. This meant continuing to dig into my being. There is always a degree of risk and pain involved when one makes the conscious decision to look at themselves with a magnifying glass. Making decisions that impact those with whom we live and love also has its own set of pain, joy and consequences.

For various reasons (excuses) I sometimes hesitate to use my divine given talents to engage in a greater work. The main one being, *If I do this what will be expected of me next? Or worse, what if I fail?* The concern of what others think of me if I fail prevailed in that conversation. While in China I did not fear failure, I just did whatever it took to get the job done. It taught me to have faith in myself, knowing a power greater than me can and will present the next steps. I am bolder now when I teach than I was before. There is less fear of someone being offended by what I say or telling me I am wrong. There are only opportunities to learn.

Fear of the Unknown

What appeared when I walked into the unknown could not be seen at first sight. If the end result had revealed itself to me it would also have shown me what it took to get there and that may have stopped me. You might think, *Wow if I knew this would happen I would have done it sooner and experienced that transformation sooner.* I don't know if that would be so. Fear of the unknown, taking risks, believing in something intangible, not being able to see, predict or control the outcomes are what I call faith. I had to have faith or belief that God had a plan and I simply had to step into it.

It takes a degree of discomfort to move into the areas of what is unfamiliar. I was at ease and comfortable being at home with my children, it was what I knew. It's almost as though I lived in a little comfort bubble. My complete focus was on our children even though it was uncomfortable when things didn't turn out the way I thought they would (or should). It was when that comfort changed into uncomfortable that I had to choose something else. I could choose to complain about my situation or change it. My new motto is *"Get comfortable with the unknown. It's where you grow."*

What's Possible?

When planting the seed of possibilities in one's heart, it germinates. As I taught my students to listen to their hearts, in turn I listened to my own. In both cases, the seeds were planted. Doubts would come and try to stop and create fear of those dreams from ever happening. But I knew my students' lives would change as they started to dream because I saw my own life change by allowing myself to dream. The students expected me to be something, which planted their belief in me. I needed to become the person who was teaching them. And I did.

One day, as I stood at the base of a large Eucalyptus tree I noticed small brown cylinder looking things on the ground. I realized they were seeds that had fallen from the tree. It is miraculous to think that a small seed evolved into such a massive, grand masterpiece. This was a witness to me that great things come from small beginnings. My experience in China was one small step that brought me to bigger things.

Choosing Myself

When I went to China I chose me. I made the decision without asking permission of anyone. I told my husband, my children and extended family I was going. I knew if I asked what they thought or if they were okay with me going I would lose power in my decision to go, and possibly let them talk me out of it.

I took a stand for my choice with conviction and responsibility, which left me feeling powerful (but nervous and scared, too). I believed in what my knowingness and true self was telling me to do and that gave me strength. Making this choice was the beginning of my self-discovery, because I listened to what my inner voice said and acted on it. I did not ask permission, or check in with others to see if they approved.

I spent many years wanting others' approval and making decisions that were based on whether they would like me or not. I sought others' validation mostly because I didn't know how to choose me, so I wanted them to choose for me. I kept looking for others to give me permission to do, go or be. After my experience in China I was convinced that I would listen to my inner voice, my compass, despite the effect it might have on others.

The whole concept of choosing me is not one I contemplated much. I didn't make room for that. Self-care didn't seem to have a place in my vocabulary or being. I thought choosing me meant someone else had to do without and I didn't want that. I considered the idea selfish, and just wrong.

Sure, when my kids were young I chose myself when it came to water and certain foods. I am a freak when it comes to having my drinking water. Every time I got in the car with my kids I told them to get their own water because I would not share mine. If there was one last chocolate chip cookie, brownie or a crisp apple, I have been known to hide it for myself. When the duties of raising and caring for the kids got too overwhelming over a period of weeks or months I would snap. I ran away to a late night movie or to sit in a parking lot alone and read a book. But I had to get to that breaking point before I let myself take care of me. I'm not saying I was a martyr (or maybe I was). I just didn't know what it was or how to choose me. My kids came first, and I wanted it that way. Dance lessons, sports, uniforms, costumes, recitals, competitions, prom dresses, school clothes, snowboard lessons, were all important to me; I wanted my kids to have the things I never had. But I have no regrets. What I saw, however, as they have left home was that I didn't know how to choose myself without feeling guilty. So I wondered *Who could I give my time and energy to.* Certainly not me!

It is this scenario that left me feeling so empty and lost when my last child left home. That is why my decision to go to China was so pivotal in my transformation. I did something for myself. Donald Miller stated in his book *A Million Miles in a Thousand Years*, "The point in life is character transformation." Little did I know that making one decision for myself would start a whole series of opportunities that led to altering my character.

Thus, the script for Act Three was being written. And the opening scene took place when I said yes to China.

What is Self-Care?

How does one learn to take care of themselves if it was forbidden (by me) or not acceptable? I was very careful and conscientious of taking care of myself in China. I had to be. To be honest I was a little afraid of getting sick and did not want to go to a hospital or doctor. It was very important for me to get exercise daily, drink water regularly, take my vitamins, meditate, not eat street food or lots of junk food (however, I did like their Magnum ice cream bars), and get rest. This was the foundation of taking care of me.

I witnessed a beautiful example of caring for something of value when I visited a man and his wife who owned a pomegranate orchard. The entire hillside was filled with pomegranate trees that were full of glorious fruit. As I approached the trees something glistened from the reflection of the sun. You might imagine my shock when I saw each individual piece of fruit on every tree wrapped in a small plastic bag tied around the stem. *What a laborious job that must have been to do this to each piece* I thought. As I sat talking (with a translator) to the orchard owner and his wife while eating the delicious fruit they shared, it was evident this orchard was their life. It was where they gave all their time and energy. They placed great value on each piece of fruit, as far as I could see every piece was tenderly wrapped. I wondered, *What if I valued myself like this fruit, and took better care of myself, would I be of more service to those around me if I did?*

As I reflected on this experience it became a revelation to me that if I wanted to serve and be a contribution to others I had to take care of me. I could teach from my higher self and be present to my students while still taking care of myself. I felt like I could make a difference in the lives of my students and still meet my own needs.

Each pomegranate was plump, juicy, and chemical- and bug-free because it was so cared for. In turn, it was of higher value to sell and delicious to eat. My realization was this: *The more I take care of myself the more I can give and share the very best I have with those around me.*

And that's what I want to do. When I take time to keep my mind, body, and spirit clear what I bring to others is a brighter presence.

What Shows Up?

Some of my personal gifts showed up while teaching in China, for example, intuition, speaking words of inspiration, energy, light and pure joy. I had seen these gifts before but would not own or acknowledge them, because I thought that might be vain. Even after seeing these gifts there were times when the fire that got ignited fizzled out and dimmed. When this happened, I would go into hiding and play small again. I had to bring myself back to my first love, the experience that brought me to see myself for the first time. When I reminded myself of what's possible and who I can be, then I was willing to play big again. I knew that beyond the fear great things were in store. I got to see my divine self and lift others in the process. I felt like I was able to boost my students into higher levels when I stepped into my own higher self. When I learned my value and that my past did not define me I could call my students out of the limitations of their own pasts and encourage them to move into bigger spaces.

How Do I Know What to Do Next?

The paths that lead us in a direction other than what we consider safe, secure, and stable are not going to be without challenges. I did not know the personal growth I would experience nor did I know how difficult it would be to leave my comforts for five weeks. My decision to go was made for me by the winch that hooked into my heart the moment I heard about this opportunity.

If you question yourself by asking, "How do I know what I am supposed to do?" simply volunteer to do things that inspire, or even scare, you. A good indication is to listen to your heart and sense its reaction when you start looking at those things. I asked for stuff to show up, told friends, family and God I was looking for something new. I was afraid to be challenged, yet I was more afraid to stay stuck in my depression.

A quote from one of my favorite books *The Little Prince* by Antoine De Saint Exupery says, "It is only with the heart that one can see rightly; what is essential is invisible to the eye." My interpretation of that quote is don't follow what you see because your eyes get tainted and skewed by lenses that are influenced from your past. Your heart is the connection to higher power and your true self. I would tell myself, *don't go AWOL to your heart, Joyce.*

Listening to the heart was a whole new concept for my students. They had been taught their whole lives to listen to their thoughts, their intellect, to figure out what they were supposed to do, and then work hard doing that. Don't get me wrong, the mind is a useful and powerful thing to have and yet using it doesn't always give us access to our true self or pathway. In my own personal life my mind is just where a whole lot of excuses and worry takes place. There aren't many answers there. If I let my mind make my decisions it is generally motivated by fear.

The decision to go to China did not involve thinking. If I thought about it I got scared and wanted to jump ship and put a stop to it. My mind can conjure up a lot of justifications when I think things over for too long. When my heart leaps or grabs onto an idea or opportunity I respond quickly. If I think it through I generally will talk myself out of it or find a reason not to do it.

When I started my blog in China it was entitled "China Blogs." Towards the completion of my first visit to China I told people "I Found Myself in China." Thus, my new blog title emerged. The reality of it is my self-discovery **began** in China, but it didn't finished there by any means. It was the beginning of a lot more responses to where my heart called me, and motivated by not getting stuck in what the mind feared.

Be Careful What You Ask For

One of the things I asked for was the gift of discernment. I wanted to know what was right, wrong, what was good for me and what wasn't, who was safe and who wasn't. Guess what I got in asking that? I had the opportunity of discerning myself and who I was and wasn't. It wasn't pretty. Suddenly I saw all my flaws and how I had judged others and made them out to be wrong only to make myself feel better about me. I felt like a fake. This query and request rocked my world for about nine months. I was pained and surprised by what I saw. I later realized that asking for that gift was just another way of me trying to control my world and its outcomes.

Listen to the Call

It was during this time of seeing my flaws (when I was not in a good place) that my friend Karen, who is a happy energetic person, reached out to me. She sent me an email on a Sunday afternoon asking if I wanted to attend a seminar with her in California. A successful woman teaching a group of entrepreneurial ladies about how to expand their knowledge in business and share their gifts led this seminar. She attached the link to what the seminar was about. I looked at it and made the immediate decision that it was not for me. I emailed her back and said, "Thanks, but I don't think it is something I want to do." She responded with, "Look again." I looked again and found that a woman speaking at the event had a nonprofit business in Ghana. I have been drawn to the thought of going to Ghana next because of my dear friend, Patience, who is from there.

Suddenly, my heart raced, my body shook, and I thought, *"I need to go and hear this woman speak."* I pulled out my calendar, the dates were clear and I was free to go. In that moment, I booked a flight to California, secured a hotel room, and then told my husband I was going. It had to be done in that order or I would've denied myself what I felt and made excuses. He was supportive and two weeks later I was in L.A.

In the email, it suggested the attire was professional. I didn't have a lot of professional-looking clothing and panicked a bit. I had a black skirt, pants and shirts that would have to suffice. I was not prepared for what I felt when I walked into that room full of women and a few men. My first thoughts were, *"You are out of your league, girl. You don't have a business; you've been nothing but a mom. You have been to China. So what? Ahhhh! RUN out of this room fast!!* It felt formal and professional when they talked about their businesses and how to expand them, as well as ways to market and create vision.

I was shocked at my immediate response of nothingness, and not belonging. We sat at round tables of eight and brainstormed on how to use what the speaker taught. I had to fake it and pretended I had a business when I didn't. I used my husband's business, which I was a part of, but it wasn't mine. At another table I talked about China like it *was* my business and I was looking to expand it and get more volunteers. I was making stuff up! My inside chatter screamed, *"Why are you here? You are such a phony! What was all that 'calling' and 'listening to your heart' crap that got you to book your plane ticket to get you here?"* I think I was expecting another awesome China experience.

The second day into the seminar (yes, I stuck it out) a guest speaker on the stage named Sheevaun Moran grabbed my heart. I loved what she had to say and it clicked. After she spoke I went up to her and asked what she did. She was a coach and I said "I need you." Her response was, "Yes, you do." At that moment, I was Humpty Dumpty fallen off the wall, broken to pieces and needed someone's help to put me back together again.

I signed up for her seminar two weeks later in L.A., loved every minute of it and hired her to be my coach. The original seminar was a catalyst to my breaking open and then seeking. Remember, when we are comfortable we resist movement or change. My discomfort pushed me to the first seminar, which created havoc inside of me and led me to my coach. It seems to be a pattern for me, but I am okay with it.

China woke me up to who I am, who I could be. Coming home pushed me into new realms of awakening. I now teach classes weekly with my husband in a business we own and partner together. We travel to California each month to see clients and continue our training and growth with our coach. I have a private practice as a coach meeting with clients individually and helping them access parts of themselves they did not know was possible or even existed. My personal growth continues daily, it never stops. I feel more alive and vibrant than I have ever felt. In January 2011 I had no idea what I felt passionate about or wanted to do. Now, I have so many things I want to do and crave constant expansion in my life.

I share this story because it is not anything that I used to do or be. Because I was up for doing and being more, I needed guidance, thus I hired a coach. My year of seeing my flaws and brokenness was a powerful awakening to seeing more of me that had been hidden way deep inside. The life I lived as a stay-at-home mom was fun and comfortable, but I was able to hide behind my kids. It was an illusion of sorts. You might say I woke up to the real world when all I could see in my reflection was me, not a bunch of others' lives dancing around mine.

It's Not a Destination, It's a Continuous Ride

Raising children, learning to help others through volunteer service, loving people, all prepared me for what was next. Each aspect of my life has been a stepping-stone for what was ahead. I would never have predicted I would go to China. It was not on my radar or in my dreams. A foundation was started when I opened my mind to help people in other countries. The experience I had was extraordinary in seeing growth in others and in me.

I had a mile marker birthday in 2016. I turned sixty! When people ask me what I will do when I retire I laugh. I am enjoying the senior citizen discounts at the movies and various stores, but there are no plans for retirement! The next phase of my life is just beginning. I went from being a dried-up streambed to a flowing rushing river. What I want to do in life is never-ending. The possibilities are infinite and I'm living with my arms wide open, heart pounding, and eyes seeing every opportunity. I actually look for the discomforts and see where they will take me. As my students would say, "I will do my best, work harder and dream bigger."

Act Three has just begun. Discovering who I am is the greatest adventure of my life, I will make sure I start the script for Act Four before it creeps up on me. Until then I'll enjoy the scenery, do hard things, appreciate what I experience and LIVE!

Acknowledgements

ACKNOWLEDGE

My life had come to a halt (or so I thought) before I met Jerrie Ueberle. She taught me about The World Academy for Women, and for that I am grateful. Her vision showed me what's possible for women in China and all over the world. Without Jerrie and this organization I would not have had the courage to go to China and have the enlightening experience that awaited me. The Academy provides an inspirational program that transforms the lives of teachers, as well as those of their students. Thank you, Jerrie, for giving me the opportunity to grow and share. And I thank all the women from the Academy for their kindness, service, love, determination and belief in miracles.

I am thankful to my friend Judi Price for sharing breakfast, introducing me to the Academy and venturing to China with me my first trip. We grew together and learned how to step into open doors of opportunity. That journey has not stopped since.

Thank you to each of my students in China and the United States for believing in your dreams and pursuing them. You are all an inspiration to me.

I'm so grateful to Steve, my husband, for his never-ending faith in me, for his encouragement and support. Thank you for sticking with and loving me through those dark nights when the resistance was real and I wanted to give up. Without your belief in me I couldn't have gone to China or written my story.

Acknowledgements

Thank you to each of our children for their love and patience in listening to my endless China stories.

A big thank you to my coach, Sheevaun Moran, for pushing me to finish and publish my ongoing, never-ending writings after putting it off for five years.

Thank you to Stacy Dymalski for being a wonderful, patient, writing coach and editor. You took me from baby steps to publication. You helped me make a story out of my blogs. All the rewrites, edits, and encouraging words kept me on task and I will be forever grateful for that. This book would not be finished without your help.

I want to acknowledge my publisher, Katie Mullaly from Surrogate Press, for walking me through each step of publication. I was definitely in the dark on this process and had no idea what to do. However, she held my hand all the way to the end and made it possible to get my story out into the public. Without you Katie, this book would have remained a bunch of edited documents in my computer. Thank you, Katie!

Thank you to Danielle Cantin for her inspired book cover. It is not what I imagined, but you saw it with your artist's eye, and I love it.

Thank you to each of my siblings, Rozanne, Karen, Lois, Dena, and Evan for cheering me on and giving me the confidence to write a book, and all my friends and family who donated money and encouragement each trip I took.

I could not have had any of these experiences without the helpers I can't see; those who let me be a conduit for the lessons and words that need to be heard by others. I want to acknowledge them for their assistance. I know in my heart that I never was, and never am, alone.

About the Author

AUTHOR

Four decades ago, Joyce Brinton graduated with a Masters in Educational Psychology from Brigham Young University. At the end of grad school, she married, found a job at Utah State Mental Hospital as a counselor, and eventually started a family. Although she loved focusing on her husband and four children, Joyce forgot who she was, what she loved, and how to take care of herself.

I Found Myself in China is the story of Joyce's search and recognition of her divine self. By unveiling her passion, she steps into who she really is, and then uses her unique gifts to create a rich community of trust. Teaching others to connect with their own dreams, she not only encourages her students to move towards their own life goals, but how to achieve those goals beyond their expectations, as well.

Joyce has a private life-coaching practice utilizing the tools of muscle testing and energy healing. A mother of four and grandmother to nine, Joyce and her husband of thirty-six years, Steve, co-teach at the Muscle Testing Academy.

Joyce is available to speak to groups of all ages about her experiences and expertise in living life more fully. Readers and listeners are instantly comfortable with her, as they learn how to create visions of their own future.

Find out more about Joyce on Facebook at: *Ifoundmyselfinchina* or you can contact her directly at *Ifoundmyselfinchina@gmail.com*.

If you would like to know more about teaching opportunities with the World Academy For The Future of Women contact Jerrie Ueberle at *jerrie@globalinteractions.org*.

www.ingramcontent.com/pod-product-compliance
Lightning Source LLC
Chambersburg PA
CBHW071528080526
44588CB00011B/1595